Super BIBLE TRIVIA FOR KIDS

BARBOUR
PUBLISHING

Fun Bible Trivia 1 © 1998 by Barbour Publishing, Inc.
Fun Bible Trivia 2 © 1999 by Barbour Publishing, Inc.

Super Bible Trivia for Kids © 2009 by Barbour Publishing, Inc.

ISBN 978-1-60260-393-6

Scripture, unless otherwise noted is taken from the King James Version of the Bible.

Scripture taken from the Good News Bible in Today's English Version copyright © 1992 by American Bible Society. Used by permission.

Published by Barbour Books, an imprint of Barbour Publishing, Inc., P.O. Box 719, Uhrichsville, Ohio 44683, www.barbourbooks.com

Our mission is to publish and distribute inspirational products offering exceptional value and biblical encouragement to the masses.

Member of the
Evangelical Christian
Publishers Association

Printed in the United States of America.

THE CREATION AND THE FALL

Genesis 1–10

1.) Who wrote the book of Genesis?

2.) What did God do on the first day?

3.) What three things did God create on the fourth day to light the universe?

4.) Did you know that gold and onyx could be found in the Garden of Eden? (Genesis 2:12)

5.) Why did Eden have a river running through it?

6.) The name of the first man was:
   a) Abraham
   b) Noah
   c) Joseph
   d) Adam

7.) Who named all of the living creatures?

8.) Why did God decide to create a woman?

9.) The name of the first woman was:
   a) Evelyn
   b) Rachel
   c) Eve
   d) Rebekah

10.) Did you know that the first woman's name means "mother of all living"? (Genesis 3:20)

11.) What did God take from Adam to make Eve?

12.) Did you know that Adam and Eve were the first married couple? (Genesis 2:23–24)

13.) The first woman was tempted by a:
   a) serpent
   b) ladybug
   c) dinosaur
   d) spider

14.) If Eve would eat the forbidden fruit, the serpent promised her:

    a) clothing

    b) riches

    c) a starring role in a movie

    d) knowledge of good and evil

15.) Did you know that Moses wrote the first five books of the Bible?

16.) After discovering their nakedness, how did Adam and Eve clothe themselves?

17.) What did Adam and Eve do when they heard God calling?

18.) When he was caught disobeying God, Adam blamed:

    a) the serpent

    b) bad programs on television

    c) Cain

    d) Eve

? ? ? ? ? ? ? ? ?

19.) After Adam and Eve ate the forbidden fruit, God:
   a) sent them out of Eden
   b) let them stay in Eden
   c) poured manna from heaven
   d) told them to build an ark so he could begin the human race again

20.) Whom did God put in place to guard the tree of life?

21.) Did you know that the first five books of the Bible are called the Pentateuch?

Genesis 4–10

1.) Who was the first son of Adam and Eve?

2.) Who was the second son born to Adam and Eve?

3.) Did you know that the slaying of Abel by Cain was the first murder?

4.) When Cain went out of the Lord's presence, he went to live in:
    a) Mod
    b) Nod
    c) Sod
    d) Cod

5.) Did you know that John Steinbeck wrote a book called *East of Eden*? This is also where Cain went to live after being exiled (Genesis 4:16).

6.) Who was Cain and Abel's brother?

7.) Who was Methuselah's father?

8.) What is mentioned twice about Enoch?

9.) Methuselah lived how many years?
    a) 30
    b) 69
    c) 90
    d) 969

10.) God told Noah to build:
    a) a yacht for Christian cruises
    b) an airplane
    c) an ark
    d) a tugboat

11.) Did you know that a cubit measures 18 inches long?

12.) How old was Noah when the flood began?

13.) One of Noah's sons was named:
    a) Ham
    b) Sham
    c) Salami
    d) Pastrami

14.) Did you know that Noah's ark was 450 feet long?

15.) What are the first five books of the Bible called?

A NEW WORLD

Genesis 11–50

1.) To reach heaven, the people tried to build:
   - a) the Empire State Building
   - b) a highway to heaven
   - c) the Tower of Babel
   - d) the Sears Building

2.) What did the Lord do when He discovered that men were trying to build a tower to reach heaven?

3.) Did you know that archaeologists discovered towers built to worship false gods in Mesopotamia?

4.) What land did Lot choose for himself when he and Abram separated?

5.) Did you know that Mohammed, the founder of the religion of Islam, was from the line of Ishmael?

6.) Hagar was:
   a) the mother of Ishmael
   b) the founder of the Haggar
      Clothing Company
   c) the mother of Abraham
   d) Sarah's neighbor

7.) When Ishmael was born, his father,
    Abram, was age:
   a) 26
   b) 36
   c) 86
   d) 96

8.) Abram's name was changed to:
   a) Lot
   b) Abraham
   c) Bam-Bam
   d) Brahma

9.) Why did God change Abram's name to
    Abraham?

? ? ? ? ? ? ? ? ?

10.) Did you know that the Hebrew word *Shaddai* is the name used for God most often in the Bible's early books?

11.) Did you know that Shaddai means "All Sufficient" or "Almighty"?

12.) Who wrote the first five books of the Bible?

13.) When God promised Abraham that his wife, Sarai, would have a baby, he:
    a) praised God
    b) invested in a college fund
    c) bought a box of expensive cigars
    d) laughed

14.) Why did Abraham give God such a response to the news?

15.) God destroyed the evil cities of:
    a) Sodom and Gomorrah
    b) Bethlehem and Nazareth
    c) London and Paris
    d) Bug Tussle and Navel Lint

16.) What happened to Lot's wife when she looked back at the cities?

17.) What was the name of Lot's wife?
    a) Marilyn Monroe
    b) Marlene Deitrich
    c) Mary Magdelene
    d) Her name is not recorded in the Bible.

18.) Did you know that the ruins of the two cities probably lie underneath the waters of the Dead Sea?

19.) Abraham and Sarah didn't want their son Isaac to marry any of the local women because they were:
    a) Canaanites
    b) Israelites
    c) members of the Electric Light Orchestra
    d) ugly

? ? ? ? ? ? ? ? ?

20.) Abraham's servant gave Rebekah:
- a) a Happy Meal
- b) Jewel Mermaid Midge
- c) silver jewelry
- d) gold jewelry

21.) How long did Jacob serve Laban before he could marry Rachel?

22.) Who was Joseph's father?

23.) Joseph's father loved him more than any of his other children because Joseph:
- a) was the child of his old age
- b) was handsome
- c) had good taste in clothes
- d) showered him with gold, frankincense, and myrrh

24.) What did Joseph's father make for Joseph?

25.) Joseph's brothers hated him even more after Joseph dreamed that:
   a) there would be a famine
   b) his brothers would serve Joseph
   c) his brothers would invent the paper clip
   d) Joseph would be the lead singer of the Partridge Family

26.) What did Joseph do during the years when there was plenty of food?

27.) What is the last event recorded in Genesis?
   a) Joseph's death
   b) Abraham's death
   c) Sarah's death
   d) Rebekah's death

? ? ? ? ? ? ? ? ?

ONE BIG EXIT
Exodus 1–37

1.) Who wrote the book of Exodus?

2.) Did you know that the word *Exodus* is from the Greek meaning *exit?*

3.) The Israelites in Egypt were:
   a) used car salesmen
   b) slaves
   c) Pharoahs
   d) rock stars

4.) The Israelites built for the Egyptians:
   a) the Tower of Babel
   b) a synagogue
   c) the Eiffel Tower
   d) treasure cities

5.) Who found the baby Moses?

6.) Where was Pharoah's daughter when she found Moses?

7.) Did you know that Moses' name is Egyptian rather than Hebrew? Egyptian Pharoahs Ramoses (Rameses) and Thutmose (Thothmes) had similar names.

8.) Moses saw an angel of God in a:
   a) microwave oven
   b) camp fire
   c) burning bush
   d) Christmas tree

9.) God promised the Israelites:
   a) forty acres and a mule
   b) a land flowing with milk and honey
   c) straw for bricks
   d) a land flowing with soda pop and potato chips

10.) Because of God's power, what could Moses turn his rod into?

11.) During the plagues, God turned the water of the Nile River into:
- a) blood
- b) wine
- c) milk and honey
- d) all the soda they could drink

12.) Did you know that the plagues were aimed against the false gods of Egypt? For example, the plague of darkness (Exodus 10:21–23) was against Ra, the Egyptian sun god.

13.) Before the Israelites left Egypt, God told them to ask for:
- a) manna
- b) milk and honey
- c) thirty shekels each
- d) silver and gold

14.) What is the Jewish observance to remember God's angel passing over their houses?

15.) What great miracle did God perform through Moses as the Israelites left Egypt?

16.) The first five books of the Bible were written by:
   a) Ezekiel
   b) Jesus
   c) Bruce Bannon
   d) Moses

17.) Were the Israelites expected to gather manna on the Sabbath?

18.) Why did God rain meat down on the wilderness?

19.) God rained what kind of meat on the wilderness for the Israelites?
   a) pigs
   b) shrimp
   c) quail
   d) cats and dogs

? ? ? ? ? ? ? ? ?

20.) On Mt. Sinai, God gave Moses:
   a) the Sermon on the Mount
   b) the Ten Commandments
   c) the Olivet Discourse
   d) manna

21.) Moses' brother was named:
   a) Aaron
   b) Joseph
   c) Fatty Z
   d) Tamar

22.) While Moses was away on Mt. Sinai, the Israelites made:
   a) gold jewelry
   b) a golden calf
   c) the first television set
   d) an army tank for protection

23.) The first five books of the Bible are called the:
   a) Pentagon
   b) Hexagon
   c) Octagon
   d) Pentateuch

24.) What other food did God provide?

25.) Who guarded the mercy seat?

STRONGMAN SAMSON

Judges 13–16

1.) Where in the Bible does Samson's story appear?

2.) What group of people ruled Israel when the book was written?

3.) Did you know that an angel appeared to Samson's mother before his birth and told her that his hair was not to be cut?

4.) The angel also told Samson's mother not to drink:
   a) 7-up
   b) manna
   c) water from the creek
   d) wine or strong drink

5.) The angel also appeared before:
   a) Samson's father, Manoah
   b) Noah
   c) Herman Munster
   d) Fred Flintstone

6.) What was the angel's name?

7.) The woman Samson wanted to marry was a:
   a) Jewess
   b) Hollywood star
   c) U.S. citizen
   d) Philistine

8.) When a lion attacked Samson after he visited the woman, he:
   a) killed it with his bare hands
   b) killed it with a slingshot
   c) made it his pet and named it Delilah
   d) ran over it with his car

9.) Inside the lion's carcass, Samson found:
   a) the sword Excalibur
   b) raspberry-flavored spring water
   c) a swarm of bees and honey
   d) granola bars

? ? ? ? ? ? ? ?

10.) What did Samson challenge his wedding banquet guests to do?

11.) The answer was given away by:
    a) an angel
    b) Samson's wife
    c) Samson's mother
    d) the TV news

12.) Because she thought Samson hated her, after the feast, Samson's wife married:
    a) Samson's friend
    b) Abraham
    c) Adam
    d) Michael Card

13.) Did you know that Samson was the thirteenth judge?

14.) Samson killed a thousand Philistines with a:
    a) dog's tail
    b) bucket of cream pies
    c) BB gun
    d) donkey's jawbone

15.) What did Samson do to make good on his promise to give thirty people fine cloaks?

16.) After the battle, God gave Samson water from:
  a) a rock
  b) the Old Faithful geyser at Yellowstone National Park
  c) a vending machine that appeared inside of a burning bush
  d) the donkey's jawbone

17.) In exchange for betraying Samson, the Philistine lords offered Delilah:
  a) 1100 pieces of silver each
  b) a nose ring
  c) a pet lizard
  d) two large ruby rings for her toes

? ? ? ? ? ? ? ? ?

18.) Did you know that Samson judged Israel for twenty years? (Judges 15:20)

19.) Did you know that if the lords were offering Delilah silver shekels, they were willing to pay about $700 each to learn about Samson?

20.) At first, Samson told Delilah that he would be weak if he were:
   a) shaven
   b) made to fast for three days
   c) tied with seven green cords of rope
   d) forced to drink nothing but fruit juice for three weeks

21.) The second time, Samson told her that he had to be tied with:
   a) silly string
   b) green yarn
   c) new rope that had never been used
   d) pieces of construction paper

22.) What did Samson tell Delilah the third time?

23.) What happened each time Samson lied to Delilah?

24.) After Samson lied to her, Delilah:
 a) gave up
 b) pestered Samson every day to tell her until he confessed
 c) lied to the Philistine lords and collected her money
 d) subbed for Vanna White as a letter turner on "Wheel of Fortune"

25.) After Samson was captured by the Philistines, what happened to his shaven hair?

26.) Did you know that Samson's head was never to be shaven because he was a Nazarite?

27.) Samson got into trouble because he:
   a) hung out with the school bullies
   b) was no longer walking with the Lord
   c) wanted Israel to have a king
   d) was out of money

28.) Why were the Philistines gathered to honor their god?

29.) How many Philistines were present at the gathering?

30.) At the gathering, Samson:
   a) told Delilah she would never have children
   b) prayed to God for strength
   c) decided to worship the god Dagon
   d) became a member of the Lions Club

31.) What happened when God granted Samson's request?

1.) Do we know who wrote the book of Ruth?

2.) Did you know that Ruth's story took place about the same time as the book of Judges?

3.) The family left home because:
   a) the wife had turned into a pillar of salt
   b) they had charged too much on their credit cards
   c) there wasn't any strawberry bubble gum in their local stores
   d) there wasn't enough food to eat because of famine

4.) Naomi and her family went to:
   a) Moab
   b) Boaz
   c) Boz
   d) Boomtown

5.) Where were Naomi and her family from?

6.) Which daughter-in-law stayed with Naomi?

7.) The women Naomi's sons married were named:
   a) Oprah Winfrey and Sally Jesse Raphael
   b) Orpah and Ruth
   c) Opie and Babe Ruth
   d) Mary and Martha

8.) How long did they live in Moab before both of Naomi's sons died?

9.) After her sons died, Naomi decided to:
   a) start a computer-consulting business
   b) open a store called Naomi's Notions
   c) stay in Moab
   d) return to her homeland

10.) After making her plans, Naomi told her daughters-in-law to:
- a) go back and live with their mothers
- b) go into business with her
- c) take care of her in her old age
- d) be sure to raise her grand-children right

11.) What happened to Naomi's husband?

12.) Did you know that the Moabites worshipped false gods? Orpah and Ruth were Moabites. Naomi told Ruth to return to her gods (Ruth 1:15).

13.) What did Ruth offer to do if Naomi would let her stay?
- a) give her a new car every year until her death
- b) keep house for her
- c) find Naomi a new husband
- d) convert to Judaism

? ? ? ? ? ? ? ?

14.) When Naomi and Ruth arrived in Bethlehem, Naomi:
   a) changed her name to Mara
   b) got a new Social Security number
   c) burned incense to Jehovah
   d) told everyone that they were following a star

15.) What grain was being harvested in Bethlehem when they arrived?

16.) What did Ruth do to provide food?

17.) Did you know that gleaning is the process of gathering up the leftover harvest in the fields? God's law allowed for the poor to glean the fields for their food (Leviticus 19:9–10).

18.) Boaz was a relative of:
   a) Naomi's husband
   b) Ruth
   c) Orpah
   d) Boyz to Men

19.) In return for gleaning only in his field, Boaz promised Ruth:
- a) that she would be safe and have plenty of water to drink
- b) three nose rings and a snake tattoo
- c) that she would be declared the most beautiful woman in Bethlehem
- d) that she could return to Moab

20.) Boaz was kind to Ruth because she:
- a) was a great beauty
- b) would soon inherit a fortune
- c) had won a $10,000,000 sweepstakes
- d) had taken good care of Naomi

21.) What two grains did Ruth glean?

22.) Does the Bible reveal the name of the kinsman Boaz told Ruth about?

23.) After the harvest season, Naomi told Ruth to:
   a) ask Boaz what to do next
   b) glean rye
   c) open a bakery since they had so much grain
   d) wear sackcloth since they would soon starve

24.) Boaz gave Ruth:
   a) six measures of barley
   b) the book *365 Ways to Serve Barley*
   c) a lecture on laziness
   d) the three nose rings and tattoo he had promised earlier

25.) What did Boaz buy on behalf of Naomi and Ruth?

26.) The kinsman wouldn't buy it because:
   a) Naomi was a Moabite
   b) Ruth was a Moabite
   c) he was a Moabite
   d) he didn't have enough money

27.) After Boaz bought the property, the elders decided to:

    a) accept Ruth as one of their own

    b) stone Ruth

    c) send her information about investments

    d) encourage her to take the money and go to college

28.) After the purchase, Boaz:

    a) asked Ruth for 10% of the money

    b) suggested that they go into the real-estate business together

    c) married Ruth

    d) sent Ruth back to Moab

29.) Did you know that the son of Ruth and Boaz was to be King David's grandfather?

30.) How many books are in the Bible?

I Samuel 1–3

1.) Did you know that I and II Samuel are considered one book in the Hebrew Bible?

2.) Hannah was upset because:
   - a) she had no children
   - b) she had no husband
   - c) she had thrown away her entry to a $10,000,000 sweepstakes
   - d) she was out of lipstick

3.) What did Hannah request of the Lord?

4.) If God answered her prayer, Hannah promised:
   - a) to become a Benedictine nun
   - b) that her son would belong to God
   - c) that she would divorce her husband
   - d) that she would go for the perfect attendance pin at church

5.) Hannah also promised the Lord that her son's hair would never be:
   a) dyed red
   b) tied with purple ribbons
   c) washed
   d) cut

6.) How did God answer Hannah's prayer?

7.) Did you know that Hannah named her son Samuel because she had asked God for him? (I Samuel 1:20).

8.) Hannah took her child to:
   a) Eli the priest
   b) Nazareth
   c) her husband
   d) an Amy Grant concert

9.) Did you know that a bullock is a young bull? Hannah's family sacrificed a bullock to the Lord before giving Samuel over to Eli the priest. (I Samuel 1:25)

? ? ? ? ? ? ? ?

10.) Why did Hannah give up her child?

11.) The sons of Eli the priest were:
   a) handsome
   b) winners of the Star Search contest
   c) evil
   d) kings

12.) As he grew, Samuel:
   a) ministered before the Lord
   b) asked to eat rich foods
   c) wanted to be more important than Abraham
   d) aced both calculus and trigonometry

13.) Each year, Hannah made Samuel a:
   a) loaf of bread
   b) videotape of all the family events he was missing
   c) little coat
   d) coat of many colors

14.) Eli the priest:
   a) blessed Hannah and her husband, Elkanah
   b) made Hannah the first woman priest
   c) gave Hannah a special portion of food
   d) promised Hannah's husband tickets to the Super Bowl

15.) How many times did the Lord call Samuel before Samuel answered the Lord, "Speak; for thy servant heareth"?

16.) Did Hannah have more children after Samuel?

17.) Did you know that Hannah was blessed by the Lord with three sons and two daughters? (I Samuel 2:21)

18.) What did God say would happen to Eli's sons?

19.) The Lord had this plan for Eli's sons because they were:
    a) evil
    b) next in line to become priests
    c) ruddy and handsome
    d) good

20.) Instead of letting Eli's sons be priests, God planned to:
    a) send Samuel to Ninevah
    b) have Samuel and Eli swallowed by a big fish
    c) shower riches and fame on Eli
    d) raise up His own priest who would do His will

21.) When God spoke to Samuel, Samuel thought he was being called by:
    a) Eli
    b) Hannah
    c) an angel
    d) the alien E.T.

22.) When Samuel was called by the Lord, Eli was:
   a) sleeping
   b) watching a prime-time soap opera
   c) trimming his toenails
   d) sacrificing a ram

23.) The Lord told Samuel He planned to:
   a) bless Eli
   b) bless Eli's sons
   c) allow Eli to win a dream house in a raffle
   d) punish Eli's house because Eli's sons were evil

? ? ? ? ? ? ? ? ?

24.) After the Lord spoke to Samuel, every-one knew Samuel would be a:
- a) lawyer
- b) prophet
- c) vegetarian
- d) hippie

25.) Did you know that the first book of Samuel was written in the tenth century before Christ?

FROM JUDGES TO A KING

I Samuel 8–10

1.) Did you know that God's people were under a government called a theocracy? That means they were ruled by God.

2.) When Samuel got old, he:
   - a) married a young woman
   - b) made his sons judges in his place
   - c) had to take antacid after every meal
   - d) refused to stop judging Israel

3.) The people were unhappy with Samuel's sons because they:
   - a) took bribes and did not rule fairly
   - b) did not exercise
   - c) had promised free education for all and then didn't build any schools
   - d) had not kept their promise of giving everyone a chicken in every pot

4.) What were the names of Samuel's two sons?

5.) Had Samuel been a good judge?

6.) Did you know that Samuel was the last of the true judges of Israel?

7.) When the people demanded a king, Samuel:
   a) was pleased
   b) prayed to the Lord
   c) gave everyone a chicken
   d) promised everyone free health benefits

8.) The Lord told Samuel to:
   a) let the people see how a king would rule
   b) sacrifice two goats and a perfect male ram
   c) produce two more sons more worthy to be judges
   d) store grain for seven years because there would be seven years of famine

9.) When the people asked for a king, whom did the Lord say they were really rejecting?

10.) Samuel warned the people that a king would be:
   a) greedy
   b) a blessing to the nation
   c) as brilliant as Albert Einstein
   d) as rich as Bill Gates

11.) Did the people heed Samuel's warning?

12.) What was the name of Israel's first king?

13.) Did you know that Saul was a descendant of the tribe of Benjamin? Saul's father was Kish; his grandfather was Abiel; his great-grandfather was Zeror, and his great-great-grandfather was a powerful Benjamite named Aphiah.

? ? ? ? ? ? ? ? ?

14.) Saul was known for:
   a) owning a red monster truck
   b) winning the pie-eating contest at the state fair five years in a row
   c) being the shortest and ugliest man in all of Israel
   d) being the tallest and most handsome man in all of Israel

15.) Saul and his servant were traveling through the country trying to find:
   a) his father's lost donkeys
   b) a Motel 6
   c) a wife for Saul
   d) jobs modeling men's fashions for the Israeli edition of *B.C. Man*

16.) Did you know that Saul and his servant planned to pay Samuel one-fourth of a silver shekel, or about 18 cents, to tell them where they could find what they were seeking? (I Samuel 9:8).

17.) Samuel knew Saul was to be the king because:
   a) God had written the message on the wall
   b) God had told Samuel in his ear that Saul was the one
   c) Samuel could feel it in his bones
   d) Samuel's left big toe always ached when he saw a king

18.) Saul was surprised that Samuel spoke to him with respect because Saul:
   a) was normally treated as stupid because he was handsome
   b) had not had a bath in three days
   c) only had 18 cents
   d) was from the smallest of the twelve tribes of Israel, and his family was not important

? ? ? ? ? ? ? ? ?

19.) What did Samuel tell Saul about his father's lost donkeys?

20.) What did Samuel do after feeding Saul dinner?

21.) Whom did they ask where to find Samuel?

22.) Did you know that another name for a prophet is a seer? (I Samuel 9:9)

23.) After Saul met the company of prophets, he had the gift of:
   a) thirty silver shekels
   b) prophecy
   c) two nose rings
   d) a chain-link fence to keep his father's donkeys from getting lost again

24.) Did everyone know right away that Saul was their new king?

YOUNG BLOOD

I Samuel 15–17

1.) Why did God reject Saul as king?

2.) Did you know that God sent Samuel to Bethlehem, the city of Jesus' birth, to find the next king? (I Samuel 16:4).

3.) Samuel thought that Eliab should be the second king because Eliab was:
   a) handsome
   b) rich
   c) planning to give Samuel money for his ministry
   d) good

4.) The Lord told Samuel that people see outward beauty, but He sees their:
   a) intelligence
   b) possessions
   c) time put in at Bible study class
   d) hearts

5.) Who was the future king's father?

6.) How many sons did Samuel see before he saw the future king?

7.) David was:
    a) short and slightly pudgy
    b) glowing with health and hand-some to look at
    c) quarterback on the football team
    d) a brainy person who wore thick glasses

8.) What did the Lord tell Samuel to do when Samuel saw David?

9.) Why did Saul want to be soothed by music?

10.) David was skillful at playing the:
    a) electric organ
    b) kazoo
    c) accordion
    d) harp

11.) Who was to be the new king of Israel?

12.) Did you know that David was the youngest son of Jesse?

13.) In Saul's court, David:
    a) loved Saul and became his armor-bearer
    b) hated Saul because David wanted to be king right away
    c) became Saul's food taster
    d) was thrown into a lion's den

14.) Who was Goliath?

15.) Did you know that Goliath's height measured six cubits and a span? A cubit measures about 21 inches, while a span measures the length of three palms of a man's hand. This means that Goliath was over 11 feet tall (I Samuel 17:4).

16.) Which of David's brothers went with Saul to battle the Philistines?

17.) While his brothers were in battle, young David:
    a) looked for his father's lost donkeys
    b) spent three days in the belly of a big fish
    c) tried out for his school's basketball team
    d) fed his father's sheep in Bethlehem

18.) How many days did Goliath taunt the Israelites?

19.) David's father sent him to visit the army to:
    a) take them food
    b) battle Goliath
    c) supply them with more bullets for their guns
    d) play the harp

20.) When David visited the army, he heard:

    a) a rousing version of "Three Blind Mice"

    b) the song "Taps" to bid the army good night

    c) an old-fashioned revival meeting

    d) Goliath's challenge to the army

21.) The person who killed Goliath was sure to get:

    a) a two-week vacation in the Bahamas

    b) a beating from Saul

    c) riches, Saul's daughter, and freedom

    d) nothing

22.) When David saw Saul, he offered to:

    a) play a polka on his harp

    b) write a new song just for Saul

    c) fight Goliath

    d) tend Saul's sheep

? ? ? ? ? ? ? ? ?

23.) To convince Saul he should fight, David said he had:

    a) won the Mr. Bodybuilder of Israel contest the previous year

    b) been the spokesman for Strong Arm Vitamins for ten years

    c) killed a lion and a bear who tried to steal his father's sheep

    d) eaten honey from the carcass of a lion who had attacked his father's sheep

24.) Whom did David think would allow him to win the battle?

25.) How many smooth stones did David select for his slingshot?

26.) The moment Goliath saw David, Goliath:

    a) ran away in fear

    b) made fun of David

    c) decided to worship the Lord

    d) asked him for skin-care tips

27.) David told Goliath that he would kill Goliath and:
   a) appear on "America's Most Wanted"
   b) that Goliath would be on "Rescue 911"
   c) everyone would know about God
   d) that David would finally get a modeling job

28.) Did you know that even though David was armed with several stones, he only used one to cause Goliath to fall to the earth? (I Samuel 17:49).

29.) What did the Philistines do after David killed Goliath?

30.) What was Eliab's reaction to seeing David at the battlefront?

THE KINGS RULE

I Kings

1.) Did you know that First and Second Kings were originally one book?

2.) What is King David like at the beginning of the first book of Kings?

3.) Adonijah was:
   a) David's father
   b) Bathsheba's son
   c) Solomon's older half-brother
   d) Solomon's stepson

4.) Adonijah declared that:
   a) he would be the next king
   b) all of his earnings would go to the homeless
   c) Israel would go back to being ruled by judges after King David's death
   d) it was time for the palace to be completely redecorated

5.) Did you know that Adonijah was David's oldest living son? The eldest son usually inherited his father's position.

6.) Did King David tell Adonijah that he would not be the next king?

7.) Adonijah was very:
   a) handsome
   b) homely
   c) nerdy
   d) geeky

8.) Who was Solomon's mother?

9.) The prophet Nathan told Solomon's mother to:
   a) speak to King David about Adonijah
   b) sacrifice a goat and two doves to the Lord
   c) burn peppermint incense until dawn
   d) crash the party

10.) Nathan was alarmed because:
    a) he hadn't eaten for two days
    b) there was to be a famine in the land
    c) he and Adonijah had argued
    d) Solomon was supposed to be the next king, not Adonijah

11.) Did King David know that Adonijah was ruling?

12.) Adonijah knew he was trying to take the throne without permission because he had not invited whom to the banquet?

13.) Did you know that Adonijah was attempting a *coup d'etat*? A coup d'etat occurs when someone takes power over a country without permission. Sometimes power is taken by force and results in war. Adonijah was trying to take power without fighting. This is called a *bloodless coup*.

14.) When King David heard that Adonijah was ruling, he:
   a) had Solomon anointed and declared king
   b) shrugged and said, "C'est la vie"
   c) lifted his scepter and said, "Carpe Diem"
   d) demanded that Adonijah's head be brought to him on a plate

15.) What animal did Solomon ride to Gihon?

16.) To celebrate, they blew a:
   a) trumpet
   b) flute
   c) piccolo
   d) kazoo

17.) Who told Adonijah the news that Solomon had been declared king?

18.) Jonathan told Adonijah and his guests that Solomon had been blessed by:
   a) Bathsheba
   b) King David
   c) Solomon
   d) the Maytag repairman

19.) How did Jonathan know this?

20.) When the guests heard the news, they:
   a) blessed Adonijah
   b) blessed Solomon
   c) asked Adonijah for doggy bags of food to take home
   d) rose up and left the party in fear

21.) After hearing the news, Adonijah:
   a) begged King Solomon not to kill him
   b) killed himself
   c) became King Solomon's food taster
   d) gave King Solomon all of his money

22.) King Solomon said that Adonijah would not die if Adonijah:
   a) promised Solomon his concubines
   b) willed Solomon his estate
   c) would live in the forest and eat locusts and wild honey
   d) proved himself worthy

23.) What would happen to Adonijah if he were wicked?

24.) Solomon said to Adonijah:
   a) "I will never forgive you."
   b) "I never want to look upon your countenance again."
   c) "This means war!"
   d) "Go to your house."

25.) Did you know that all of Judah's kings were from the line of David?

1.) Did you know that God is not mentioned by name in the book of Esther?

2.) The king became angry with Queen Vashti because she:
   a) was ugly
   b) had too many bills on her credit cards
   c) disobeyed him
   d) made more money than he did

3.) Because of his anger with Queen Vashti, the king decreed that:
   a) men with quick tempers should join a twelve-step program
   b) women were to honor men and men were to rule their households
   c) men could have as many as 300 wives
   d) the Equal Rights Amendment should be passed

4.) Why did the king want the people to see Queen Vashti?

5.) Why were all of the fair maidens brought before the king?

6.) Did you know that the name Esther means *star*?

7.) Mordecai was what relation to Esther?
- a) cousin
- b) financial advisor
- c) mutual-fund manager
- d) study partner

8.) Mordecai treated Esther as his daughter because:
- a) she was lovely
- b) she was an orphan
- c) she worked for him
- d) he hoped to get her a part on a television soap opera

? ? ? ? ? ? ? ?

9.) The book of Esther was written by:
   a) Moses
   b) Jesus
   c) R.L. Stine
   d) We don't know.

10.) What did the king do when Esther found favor with him?

11.) What had Esther not revealed about herself when she won the contest?

12.) Why didn't Esther reveal her secret?

13.) Mordecai saved the king's life by:
   a) throwing him a life preserver from the sinking ship, *Titanic*
   b) telling him through Esther that his life was in danger from assassins
   c) catching a radio before it landed in his bathwater
   d) warning him about a frayed bungee cord

14.) Mordecai refused to bow to Haman because Mordecai:
   - a) was Jewish
   - b) had arthritis
   - c) was a member of a cult that believed in UFOs
   - d) wanted payment to bow to Haman

15.) What did Haman plan to do to all the Jews?

16.) Did you know that the Jews were bought by Haman for 10,000 silver talents?
   If:
   I shekel = 64 cents,
   I mina = 50 shekels, and
   I talent = 60 minas,
   then the total price Haman offered for the Jews was: $19,200,000.

? ? ? ? ? ? ? ? ?

17.) To replace his sackcloth, Esther sent Mordecai:
- a) a lynx coat
- b) a bearskin rug
- c) designer blue jeans
- d) fine raiment

18.) Why didn't Esther want to speak to the king on her people's behalf?

19.) Esther asked the Jews to do what before she spoke to the king?
- a) fast for three days and nights
- b) sacrifice a ram in her honor
- c) hold another beauty contest
- d) will all of their money to her

20.) When she threw the banquet where she would speak to the king, Esther also invited:
- a) Jesus
- b) Adam
- c) DC Talk
- d) Haman

21.) The king read his records and discovered Mordecai's good deed because the king:
  - a) couldn't sleep
  - b) was sick in bed with chicken pox
  - c) was looking for something to do while waiting for brownies to bake
  - d) wanted to read while having his toenails painted

22.) What did the king decide to do for Mordecai for saving his life?

23) After Haman's death, the king gave Mordecai a:
  - a) ring
  - b) season pass to the nearest amusement park
  - c) coupon for a free tattoo
  - d) coat of many colors

? ? ? ? ? ? ? ? ?

24.) Whom did Haman think the king wanted to honor?

25.) At the banquet, whom did Esther reveal was the enemy?

26.) To show Esther that her life had been spared, the king:
    a) tapped her on the shoulder with his sword
    b) held a golden scepter toward her
    c) bought her a Newsboys CD
    d) gave her a ring

27.) What holiday was established to remember this event?

28.) Did you know that the Jews still celebrate this holiday?

29.) According to the book of Esther, when should the holiday be observed?

30.) Did you know that the Hebrew month of Adar is February through March on our calendar?

A FAITHFUL SERVANT

Job

1.) Did you know that there are three Wisdom Books in the Bible? They are Job, Proverbs, and Ecclesiastes. Wisdom books deal with human experience through sayings, essays, monologues, or drama.

2.) Where did Job live?
   - a) Uz
   - b) Buzz
   - c) Fuzz
   - d) Scuzz

3.) How many children did Job have?

4.) If God took away Job's possessions, Satan said Job would:
   - a) praise God
   - b) make more money
   - c) start a company called Job's Jobs
   - d) curse God

5.) The Lord told Satan that he must:
   a) give Job back his possessions
   b) raise his children from the dead
   c) turn water into wine
   d) spare Job's life

6.) Satan afflicted Job with painful:
   a) headaches
   b) tax audits from the Internal Revenue Service
   c) sores
   d) bunions

7.) Job's wife advised him to:
   a) will his possessions to her before he died
   b) curse God and die
   c) go on an herbal diet
   d) remain faithful to God

8.) Job was visited by whom during his suffering?

9.) To make peace with Him, what did the Lord command Job's visitors to do?

10.) Job's visitors tried to:
- a) comfort Job
- b) teach him computer skills so he could find a new job
- c) convince him to divorce his wife
- d) run his farm while he was sick

11.) The Lord told Job's visitors that He was:
- a) pleased with them
- b) willing to prosper them
- c) angry that they were unsuccessful at teaching Job new skills
- d) angry about their unfaithfulness to Him

12.) How many years did Job live after his test?

13.) After Job's suffering, God:
   a) gave him twice as much as he had before his suffering
   b) gave him three times as much as he had before his suffering
   c) gave him four times as much as he had before his suffering
   d) allowed Job to win both show-cases on *The Price is Right*

14.) God restored unto Job:
   a) three daughters and seven sons
   b) seven daughters and three sons
   c) ten beautiful daughters
   d) ten handsome sons

15.) Job's new daughters were renowned for their:
   a) wealth
   b) intelligence
   c) victory on *It's Academic*
   d) beauty

BITS OF WISDOM

Proverbs

1.) Solomon was:
   a) a king of Israel
   b) one of the twelve disciples
   c) David's father
   d) a writer for popular TV
      programs

2.) Who is the giver of wisdom?

3.) A wise person runs away from:
   a) a pesky younger brother
   b) chores
   c) Dad when there's a bad report card
   d) evil

4.) When the Lord loves you, He:
   a) shows you right from wrong
   b) gives you money beyond your
      dreams
   c) won't let you get chicken pox
   d) will make sure your homework
      gets done

5.) Happy is the person who finds what?

6.) We should be like ants because they:
    a) work
    b) steal picnic food
    c) are pretty
    d) are quiet

7.) Proverbs lists how many things that the Lord hates?
    a) six
    b) seven
    c) sixty-six
    d) seventeen

8.) Proverbs cautions against:
    a) having too many wives
    b) bad women
    c) letting women talk you into going to a boring party
    d) letting your wife have her way

9.) Did you know that the book of Proverbs was put together in the tenth century before Christ?

10.) You should think of wisdom as your:
   a) mother
   b) daughter
   c) fiancée
   d) sister

11.) Did you know that when the author of Proverbs says to call wisdom your sister, it means that you should hold wisdom in high regard? You can also think of it as walking hand in hand with wisdom, a cherished virtue.

12.) Wisdom is better than:
   a) cherry bubble gum
   b) winning the lottery
   c) rubies
   d) the prizes in Happy Meals

13.) Who wrote the book of Proverbs?

14.) Did you know that a proverb is a wise saying?

15.) What is the theme of the book of Proverbs?

16.) When you tell a wise person about a mistake, the person will:
   a) laugh at you
   b) love you
   c) hate you
   d) gossip about you

17.) Why does a wise person welcome correction?

18.) According to Proverbs, will wisdom make you live longer?

19.) Hatred stirs anger, but sin is covered by:
   a) hate
   b) anger
   c) love
   d) slime

20.) Does the book of Proverbs advise against gossip?

21.) Why do you think the author of Proverbs would say not to speak badly of others?

22.) A person who will not listen to wise advice will find:
   a) poverty and shame
   b) health and wealth
   c) his own wisdom
   d) a walk-on part on *Saved by the Bell*

23.) A person who heeds wise advice will find:
   a) shame
   b) a winning lottery ticket
   c) honor
   d) fame

24.) What can you do to make someone less angry?

25.) Pleasant words are like a:
   a) sword
   b) spear
   c) sweet potato pie
   d) honeycomb

26.) What is the crown of an old man?

27.) According to Proverbs, we will be punished if we:
   a) tell lies
   b) beat up the school bully
   c) spend too much time playing computer games
   d) make bad grades in school

28.) Did you know that even a child will be known by his doings? (Proverbs 20:11).

29.) What does Proverbs 20:23 mean by saying a false balance is not good?

30.) Why shouldn't you give good advice to a foolish person?

31.) We shouldn't be jealous of wicked people because they:
   a) will have no reward
   b) will be cursed
   c) know the Lord
   d) will get fat from eating too much rich food

32.) If you are rich, you should:
   a) buy at least three vacation homes
   b) star in a Hollywood movie
   c) eat at the White House with the president
   d) only buy as many things as you need and no more

33.) What would Solomon say about the advertising slogan, "Diamonds are forever"?

34.) If your enemy is hungry, you should:
   a) throw a cream pie in his face and laugh
   b) not let him near your parties because he'll eat everything in sight
   c) give him bread to eat
   d) give a donation in his name to the nearest soup kitchen

35.) Did Solomon say it is okay to insult each other as long as it's all in fun?

36.) How would Solomon know about riches?

37.) You will always have enough money if you:
   a) save all of your money
   b) invest in a company called Solomon's Secure Stocks
   c) borrow money from other people but don't pay it back
   d) give to the poor

38.) An angry man:
   a) is a victim of his surroundings
   b) should be put on the welfare rolls
   c) stirs up even more anger
   d) should be allowed to get away with anything he wants

39.) How many books are in the Old Testament?

40.) Did you know that the Bible has a total of sixty-six books?

THE GOOD WIFE

Proverbs

1.) A good woman is:
   a) virtuous
   b) beautiful
   c) rich
   d) skinny

2.) What is a virtue?

3.) A good woman is more valuable than what?

4.) Her husband can trust his wife with his:
   a) pet hamster
   b) credit cards
   c) heart
   d) car

5.) What two things does the Proverbs 31 woman seek?

6.) Who gives honor to the good wife?

7.) When it is time to work, she:
  a) passes off her chores to her children
  b) hires the best maid in town
  c) works willingly
  d) calls her mother on the phone and complains

8.) Where does the Proverbs 31 woman get food?

9.) The Proverbs 31 woman starts her day:
  a) before dawn
  b) after she's caught up on all the latest gossip
  c) noon
  d) as soon as her children get in from school

10.) What virtue is described in Proverbs 31:14–19?

? ? ? ? ? ? ? ? ?

11.) The virtue of giving to the poor is called:
   a) flattery
   b) deceit
   c) guile
   d) charity

12.) She is not afraid of snow because:
   a) it gives her a chance to rent videos and eat microwave popcorn all day
   b) she has plenty of clothing to keep her family warm
   c) she has a four-wheel-drive vehicle
   d) the central heating system in her house is always working

13.) What color does the Proverbs 31 woman wear?

14.) Did you know that purple was once worn only by very rich people? In Bible times, purple dye came from a shellfish that could only produce a little color at a time, so the dye was very expensive.

15.) What does the virtuous woman sell?

16.) A good wife wears:
    a) a frown on her face
    b) plenty of red lipstick
    c) only the latest sneakers
    d) strength and honor

17.) When a good woman speaks, what do her words have?

18.) Beauty is not the first concern of the Proverbs 31 woman because she:
    a) already sold her stock in Revlon
    b) is too old to be a model
    c) is not vain or conceited
    d) is vain and conceited

19.) What is more important than beauty in a good woman?

20.) What will happen to the woman who fears the Lord?

DREAM WEAVER

Daniel

1.) Who wrote the book of Daniel?

2.) Did you know that the book of Daniel is called an *apocalypse*? Apocalypse means "unveiling." The book of Daniel shows that good will win over evil.

3.) When Daniel had a chance to eat the rich foods of King Nebuchadnezzar, he asked:
    a) for second helpings
    b) a doggy bag
    c) for Pharoah's own steak sauce for his Beef Wellington
    d) to be excused from eating food forbidden under Jewish dietary laws

4.) When the Lord heard Daniel's request not to eat the king's food, what did the Lord grant Daniel?

5.) What special talent did God give to Daniel that would later help the king?

6.) Did you know that the book of Daniel was written in the Aramaic language?

7.) What did King Nebuchadnezzar say should happen to his wise men when they couldn't interpret his dream?

8.) When King Nebuchadnezzar asked Daniel to interpret his dream, Daniel:
    a) asked the king for more time and prayed to God for wisdom
    b) told the king about the dream right away
    c) asked for more of the king's rich food
    d) presented him with a contract asking for blue M&M candies

9.) King Nebuchadnezzar made an image of what kind of metal?

? ? ? ? ? ? ? ? ?

10.) Did you know that the image King Nebuchadnezzar made was 90 feet high? (Daniel 3:1).

11.) Anyone who refused to worship the image would be:
    a) honored by King Nebuchadnezzar
    b) granted the king's daughter's hand in marriage
    c) thrown into a fiery furnace
    d) given extra money to buy Warheads candy

12.) After the king dreamed of a tree, he:
    a) went to live with the beasts of the field, eating grass for food
    b) became a forest ranger for the U.S. Park Service
    c) walked around the country with a pot on his head, planting apple seeds
    d) ate wild locusts and honey

13.) Did you know that the king had given Daniel the name Belteshazzar? (Daniel 5:12).

14.) What did King Belshazzar do at his banquet to offend God?

15.) God communicated to King Belshazzar:
   a) with handwriting on a wall
   b) through a burning bush
   c) through the U.S. Post Office
   d) by appearing on TV

16.) Who was the only person who could interpret the handwriting?

17.) Who told King Belshazzar to see Daniel?

18.) Did Daniel's friends worship the image?

19.) What happened when the three Hebrews were thrown into the fiery furnace?

20.) Did you know that many of the dreams and visions recorded in the book of Daniel predict events that *still* have not taken place?

THE UNWILLING SERVANT

Jonah

1.) Who wrote the book of Jonah?

2.) Did you know that Jonah was the first foreign missionary?

3.) Where did God tell Jonah to go?

4.) Jonah went to:
    a) Ninevah
    b) Tarshish
    c) Joppa
    d) Cleveland

5.) Jonah tried to hide:
    a) on *The Love Boat*
    b) on a ship heading to Tarshish
    c) at the home of Johnny Quest
    d) under his bed

6.) Did you know that the name Jonah means "dove"?

7.) What did God send out that frightened the people on the ship?

8.) As Jonah slept on the ship, the others called out to:
   a) their gods
   b) Jehovah
   c) a UFO they spotted
   d) a news van from a local TV station

9.) Since he had put them in danger, Jonah told the others to:
   a) be sure they had plenty of food
   b) interpret his dream from the night before
   c) convert to Jonah's faith
   d) throw him overboard

10.) Did they throw Jonah overboard right away?

11.) Did you know that the Bible does not say that Jonah was swallowed by a whale, but a great fish? (Jonah 1:17).

12.) After Jonah was thrown overboard, the sea:
    a) grew even rougher
    b) made big waves for the surf dudes to ride
    c) parted
    d) grew calm

13.) What did Jonah do while he was inside the fish?

14.) After the fish vomited Jonah onto dry land, the Lord told Jonah to:
    a) take a bath
    b) go to Ninevah
    c) return home
    d) apologize to the men on the ship

15.) Did you know that the city of Ninevah was so large that it took three days to walk all the way around it? (Jonah 3:3).

16.) How long was Jonah inside the fish?

17.) What was Jonah's message to Ninevah from God?

18.) Upon hearing the message, the people of Ninevah:
    a) fasted and wore sackcloth
    b) ate a big turkey dinner and put on Pilgrim costumes
    c) ate only chocolate and wore only purple for three days
    d) celebrated Lent

19.) When the king of Ninevah heard the message, he sat in:
    a) his throne
    b) the third-row seat of the movie theater
    c) ashes
    d) the city dump

20.) What happened when God saw that the citizens of Ninevah had repented?

21.) Did you know that the repentance of Ninevah is the biggest revival known to man?

22.) When the city repented, Jonah:
   a) rejoiced
   b) was angry
   c) threw a big party
   d) was the guest of honor at a big banquet given by the king

23.) Did you know that Jonah 4:2 gives us clues about God's character? In this verse, Jonah describes God as gracious, merciful, slow to anger, and kind.

24.) Why did Jonah want to stay near Ninevah?

25.) For shelter, God gave Jonah a:
   a) beautiful mansion
   b) sunflower
   c) mobile home
   d) gourd

? ? ? ? ? ? ? ? ?

26.) How did Jonah feel after God took away his shelter?

27.) By killing the plant Jonah loved, what lesson did God teach Jonah?

28.) Did you know about 120,000 people lived in Ninevah? (Jonah 4:11).

29.) The Bible has:
   a) six books
   b) sixteen books
   c) sixty-six books
   d) six hundred books

30.) Did you know that there are thirty-nine books in the Old Testament?

Matthew

1.) Who wrote the book of Matthew?

2.) Did you know that Matthew was a tax collector?

3.) The book of Matthew starts by recording:
    a) Jesus' birth
    b) the creation
    c) St. Paul's birth
    d) Jesus' birth line, or genealogy

4.) Did you know that it was unusual for birth records to mention women, although Matthew mentions them in his gospel?

5.) In what city was Jesus born?

6.) Did you know that the King Herod of Jesus' time was known as Herod the Great?

7.) King Herod sought the baby Jesus to:
   a) worship Him
   b) give Him gold, frankincense, and myrrh
   c) give Mary and Joseph money for a hotel room at Embassy Suites
   d) kill Jesus

8.) To keep Him safe from Herod, Mary and Joseph took Jesus to:
   a) Egypt
   b) Uz
   c) Edom
   d) Paris

9.) The food John the Baptist ate was:
   a) manna
   b) cookies made by elves
   c) milk and honey
   d) locusts and wild honey

10.) Did you know that all of the Gospels record the ministry of John the Baptist?

11.) How long was Jesus tempted by the devil?

12.) What would Peter and Andrew fish for if they followed Jesus?

13.) Another name for Jesus' Sermon on the Mount is:
    a) Beatitudes
    b) Attitude Adjustments
    c) Beatniks
    d) Assertiveness Training

14.) Did you know that the comparisons of Christians to salt and light are called similitudes?

15.) What do we call the prayer Jesus taught His disciples?

16.) Jesus said to store your treasures in:
    a) the stock market
    b) mutual funds
    c) real estate
    d) heaven

? ? ? ? ? ? ? ? ?

17.) Did you know that in New Testament times, a worker earned about sixteen cents a day?

18.) What do we call Jesus' command to do to others as you would have them do to you?

19.) The relative of Peter's whom Jesus healed was Peter's:
   a) second-cousin twice removed
   b) kissin' cousin
   c) step-great-grandmother
   d) mother-in-law

20.) What is another name for the stories Jesus used to teach people?

21.) How many disciples did Jesus call?

22.) When the disciples saw Jesus walking on the water, they thought He was a:
   a) ghost
   b) hologram
   c) hallucination
   d) mirage

23.) Jesus healed the Canaanite woman's daughter because of her:
   a) great faith
   b) gift of gold, frankincense, and myrrh
   c) desire to wash His feet with perfume
   d) gift of a video game set and several cartridges

24.) Did Jesus know He was to be crucified?

25.) We should be watchful because:
   a) someone might steal our treasures
   b) we don't know when the Lord will return
   c) we might have forgotten to turn on our security systems
   d) our watchdog is at the vet

26.) Which disciple agreed to betray Jesus?

27.) Jesus was betrayed in exchange for:
   a) nothing
   b) tickets to a concert
   c) the widow's mite
   d) thirty pieces of silver

28.) What was the name of the garden where Jesus prayed before His crucifixion?

29.) When Jesus asked His disciples to watch with Him as He prayed, they:
   a) slept
   b) obeyed
   c) ate the leftover bread and fish from the lunch Jesus fed the 5,000
   d) played Uno

30.) Judas betrayed Jesus with the following sign:
   a) cutting off His right ear with a sword
   b) kissing Him
   c) denying Him three times
   d) offering Him a meal of locusts and wild honey

31.) After Judas betrayed Jesus, he:
    a) repented
    b) spent his money on video
       rentals
    c) went into the Federal Witness
       Protection Program
    d) was interviewed on the news
       program *20/20*

32.) Did you know that Judas's betrayal of Jesus is told in all of the Gospels?

33.) What did the centurion say when the earth quaked at Jesus' crucifixion?

34.) The stone on the door of Jesus' tomb was rolled back by:
    a) Judas
    b) Mary Magdalene
    c) Pharoah
    d) an angel

? ? ? ? ? ? ? ?

35.) The risen Jesus said He would meet His disciples at:
   a) Galilee
   b) His mother's house for pizza
   c) Smokey Joe's Cafe
   d) the Bethlehem drive-in theater

36.) Where did Jesus tell Peter to get money for taxes?

37.) Did you know that the penny (denarius) Jesus mentions in Matthew 20:2 was the most common coin at that time?

38.) Why didn't the soldiers on watch at the tomb admit that the Son of God had risen?

39.) What does Jesus' resurrection prove?

40.) What is the last word in the book of Matthew?

JOHN'S JOURNEY WITH JESUS

John

1.) Who wrote the book of John?

2.) Did you know that the book of John does not record the events surrounding Jesus' birth?

3.) Where did Jesus perform His first miracle?
    a) Cane
    b) Cain
    c) Cana
    d) Cathy

4.) Who told Jesus there was no more wine?

5.) The event where Jesus performed His first miracle was a:
    a) circus
    b) bar mitzvah
    c) wedding
    d) birthday party

6.) Did you know that the author of the book of John was one of Jesus' twelve disciples?

7.) When Jesus saw the moneychangers at the temple, He:
    a) bought three doves and two goats
    b) asked for change for the vending machines
    c) asked what time the Bible study on the book of Revelation would occur
    d) overturned their tables and angrily rebuked them

8.) God promises believers:
    a) earthly riches
    b) eternal life
    c) manna
    d) a year's supply of Rice a Roni, the San Francisco treat

9.) What did Jesus ask the woman at the well to give Him?

10.) What important news did Jesus tell the woman about Himself?

11.) Jesus fed a large crowd of people with:
   a) five barley loaves and two small fish
   b) three cans of soda and a pack of M&Ms
   c) five candy bars and a pint of lemonade
   d) five coffee beans and a peanut butter and jelly sandwich

12.) How many people were in the crowd?

13.) Jesus was betrayed by:
   a) Judas Iscariot
   b) Moses
   c) Pharoah
   d) James Bond, Agent 007

14.) What did Jesus do to serve His disciples at the Last Supper?

15.) What lesson did this teach the disciples?

16.) Did you know that Jesus showed He knew who would betray Him by giving Judas bread dipped in wine?

17.) Did Jesus know that Peter would deny Him three times?

18.) Immediately after Peter had denied Jesus three times, a:
   a) donkey brayed
   b) fire engine siren went off
   c) rooster crowed
   d) woman screamed

19.) Did you know that all four Gospels tell us about Peter's denial of Jesus?

20.) When Pilate presented Jesus to the mob during Passover, they cried:
   a) "He is our king!"
   b) "Have mercy on Him!"
   c) "For He's a jolly good fellow!"
   d) "Crucify Him!"

21.) What will we do if we love Jesus?

22.) What did the sign Pilate made for Jesus' cross say?

23.) Did you know that Pilate's sign was written in Hebrew, Greek, and Latin? (John 19:20)

24.) What did Jesus say as He died on the cross?

25.) The angels at Jesus' tomb said to Mary Magdalene:
   a) "Why weepest thou?"
   b) "Fetch us something to eat."
   c) "We know you have been married five times."
   d) "Why are there so many women named Mary in the Bible?"

26.) What did the risen Jesus say to Mary Magdalene?

? ? ? ? ? ? ? ? ?

27.) Did Thomas believe the disciples when they said they had seen the risen Christ?

28.) The fact that Jesus rose from the dead proves that Jesus is:
    a) a good teacher
    b) a religious leader
    c) really, really smart
    d) the Son of God, who is worthy to be worshipped

29.) John says he wrote his book so you will:
    a) feed the poor
    b) be healthy, wealthy, and wise
    c) be a good person
    d) believe in Jesus Christ, the Son of God, and have life in His name

30.) What is the last word in the book of John?

NEWS FOR THE ROMANS

Paul's Epistle to the Romans

1.) Who wrote the Epistle to the Romans?

2.) The letter was written to:
    a) Roman Christians
    b) Caesar
    c) the owner of Roma Restaurant
    d) the Vatican Council

3.) Did you know that the letter to the Romans was written almost sixty years after Jesus was crucified?

4.) The letter is written about:
    a) Roman Christians
    b) the Vatican Council
    c) why they should give Paul money for his mission work
    d) Jesus Christ our Lord, the Son of God

5.) What proof does Paul offer that Jesus is holy?

6.) Did you know that the term "saint" applies to any Christian? Paul tells the Roman Christians that they are called to be saints (Romans 1:7).

7.) We can have peace with God through:
   a) random acts of kindness
   b) helping an old lady cross the street every day
   c) making sure we give 10% of our allowance to church every Sunday
   d) faith in our Lord Jesus Christ

8.) To receive salvation, we have to pay Jesus:
   a) by being ministers and missionaries when we grow up whether we want to or not
   b) by spending at least an hour a day reading the Bible
   c) by ignoring people who tease us
   d) nothing. His gift of salvation is free.

9.) Who makes us righteous?

10.) Did you know that the old man Paul talks about is our old nature that wants to sin? (Romans 6:6).

11.) Christians live under grace instead of having to follow laws. This is called:
   a) the New Covenant
   b) the Declaration of Independence
   c) the Apostles' Creed
   d) the Girl Scout Pledge

12.) Once you stop living for sin, you are guided by:
   a) your minister
   b) your Sunday School teacher
   c) your friends
   d) the Holy Spirit

13.) What two things will you find if you live in the Spirit?

? ? ? ? ? ? ? ? ?

14.) Is any person righteous without Jesus?

15.) When a Christian is too sad or upset to pray, what does the Holy Spirit do?

16.) When we pray, whose plan shall be carried out?
   a) ours
   b) God's
   c) our pastor's
   d) our parents'

17.) We can be separated from God's love by:
   a) not going to church every Wednesday and Sunday
   b) bad people
   c) too much television
   d) nothing

18.) What does Paul mean when he writes: "Even us, whom he hath called, not of the Jews only, but also of the Gentiles"?

19.) Did you know that the Gentiles were the unbelievers of Bible times?

20.) Which one of the twelve tribes of Israel was Paul from?

21.) Paul said he was Jewish so the Roman Christians would know that:
    a) God has not forgotten His chosen people
    b) Paul was better than the Roman Christians
    c) Paul had paid handsomely to have a professional trace his family line
    d) Paul was eligible to be a member of the Boy Scouts

22.) The Romans were:
    a) Jewish
    b) Catholic
    c) Gentiles
    d) popular

23.) Paul wrote that he was an apostle of whom?

24.) Did you know that in this letter Paul gives us a clue as to God's character? He describes God as possessing matchless knowledge and wisdom (Romans 11:33).

25.) As to our gifts from God, Paul said:
    a) all Christians have equal gifts
    b) we should go to classes to develop our gifts
    c) that for a small fee, he would help the Romans find their gifts
    d) we should use whatever gifts God gave us

26.) Who is in charge of seeking revenge for evil?

27.) Evil will be overcome by:
    a) evil
    b) cutting others down
    c) the sword
    d) good

28.) Who will judge all of us?

29.) What is the last word in this letter?

THE THESSALONIANS

I and II Thessalonians

1.) Who wrote the epistles to the Thessalonians?

2.) The name of the place where the Thessalonians lived was:
   a) Thesis
   b) Thessalonica
   c) Toronto
   d) Thessa

3.) Did you know that the epistles to the Thessalonians were written in AD 51?

4.) The group of Thessalonians Paul was writing to was the:
   a) church
   b) people who would finance his retirement
   c) pagans
   d) Gentiles

5.) Did you know that an epistle is a letter?

6.) After greeting the Thessalonians, Paul:
   a) praises them
   b) asks for a love offering
   c) tells them to start a Bible college
   d) tells them not to buy a Cadillac when a Ford would serve their purpose

7.) Paul tells them that when they talk they should:
   a) not offend anyone
   b) be sure they are recorded on videotape
   c) not forget to ask for money
   d) worry about pleasing God, not people

8.) Whom did Paul say tried to keep him from making progress?

9.) Did you know that the word *edify* means to teach, educate, or guide spiritually? Paul says that Christians should edify each other (I Thessalonians 5:11).

10.) Paul tells the Thessalonians to:
  a) love one another
  b) take turns with the household chores
  c) carry swords at all times
  d) vote Republican

11.) Paul says that Christians should put on:
  a) cosmetics that have not been tested on animals
  b) a happy face
  c) the breastplate of faith and love and a helmet of hope and salvation
  d) army uniforms

12.) What else did Paul tell us to do in I Thessalonians 5:11?

13.) What did Paul say to do without ceasing?

14.) Paul said never to seem:
   a) evil
   b) too friendly to the pagans
   c) unwilling to share
   d) uncool

15.) The last word in the first letter to the Thessalonians is:
   a) "Hello."
   b) "G'day."
   c) "Godspeed."
   d) "Amen."

? ? ? ? ? ? ? ? ?

HEBREWS

1.) Who wrote the Epistle to the Hebrews?

2.) Did you know that twenty-one books of the New Testament are epistles?

3.) An epistle is a:
    a) letter
    b) book
    c) novel
    d) wife of an apostle

4.) Today, God speaks to us:
    a) through a megaphone
    b) by playing recordings backwards
    c) by appearing in a burning bush
    d) through His Son Jesus

5.) Whom does the author of Hebrews trust?

6.) As the perfect Son of God, what does Jesus offer to all who obey Him?

7.) What are angels?

8.) If we accept Jesus, we will find:
   a) a way to make good grades in school
   b) mercy and grace
   c) a lot of money
   d) many friends

9.) Good deeds are not as important to the Christian as:
   a) faith
   b) voting
   c) having more video games than anyone else
   d) being the most popular person in school

10.) What does God think of good works done in His name?

11.) Did you know that today Christians live under the New Covenant described in Hebrews? The old Mosaic covenant meant that God's people followed a set of rules. Under the New Covenant,

Jesus died for our sins. We are forgiven if we accept Jesus as our personal Savior (Hebrews 8:12–13).

12.) To please God, a Christian must have:
   a) given up chocolate for Lent
   b) gone to vacation Bible school every year for five years
   c) a wardrobe of Christian T-shirts and at least ten CDs by Christian musicians
   d) faith

13.) Name at least two people of faith described in Hebrews.

14.) Where is Jesus now?

15.) What is the last word of the letter to the Hebrews?

16.) Instead of burnt offerings, what sacrifice should we offer to God?

17.) God corrects us because He:
   a) will benefit
   b) wants all Christians to be mis-
      sionaries to the North Pole
   c) wants us to learn how to be
      holy
   d) thinks it is fun

18.) No one will see God without:
   a) a certificate of baptism
   b) permission from St. Peter at the
      pearly gates
   c) teaching Sunday school for
      twenty years
   d) holiness

19.) Some have entertained strangers who
were really:
   a) angels
   b) St. Paul
   c) St. Peter at the pearly gates
   d) members of Michael W. Smith's
      band

20.) Why should we ignore strange
teachings?

JOHN'S LETTERS

I, II, and III John

1.) What is an epistle?

2.) How many epistles did John write?

3.) The Epistles of John were written by:
   a) John the Baptist
   b) Jonathan Pierce
   c) Jonathan Taylor Thomas
   d) John the Apostle

4.) If we say we have no sin, we are fooling:
   a) ourselves
   b) our parents
   c) our teachers
   d) our friends

5.) Did you know that when John writes about little children, he means all Christians?

6.) What commandment does John repeat?

7.) To show us His love, God:
   a) sent His only begotten Son into the world, that we might live through Him
   b) sent manna to all Christians
   c) promised vast wealth to all Christians
   d) promised that one day we would have pictures of Mars

8.) Throughout his first letter, John tells Christians not to love:
   a) their brothers
   b) pagans
   c) television
   d) the world

9.) John says that true Christians have:
   a) love
   b) fear
   c) gold plaques with their names engraved on them
   d) money invested in John's real-estate firm

10.) How does John define God?

11.) What will happen to those who say that Jesus is the Son of God?

12.) Whom will you love if you also love God?

13.) Did you know that I John 5:7 was probably not written by John, but added later?

14.) John tells the little children to stay away from:
   a) bad movies
   b) cereal with too much sugar
   c) violent video games
   d) idols

15.) What is the last word in John's first letter?

16.) Did you know that the elect lady John speaks of in his second letter is probably another name for a church?

17.) What three blessings does John wish his readers?

18.) John says that when someone pretends to be a Christian but really isn't, you should:
   a) not let the person into your house
   b) pretend you don't speak English
   c) spread the blood of a lamb on your door
   d) tell everybody at school

19.) Why does John say you should not wish a false Christian well?

20.) Why is John's second letter short?

21.) The final word in John's second epistle is:
   a) "Adios."
   b) "Bonjour."
   c) "Cheerio."
   d) "Amen."

22.) Did you know that John's third letter is written to his friend Gaius?

23.) What blessings did John wish Gaius?

24.) Gaius was:
  a) a strong Christian who walked in the truth
  b) a pagan John was trying to convert
  c) one of the twelve disciples
  d) a rich merchant who gave John millions of dollars to run his ministry

25.) John was angry with Diotrephes because Diotrephes:
  a) was more concerned about his reputation than he was about other Christians
  b) refused to let John marry his daughter
  c) did not offer John snails cooked in garlic sauce for dinner
  d) made corrections to John's second epistle with red ink

? ? ? ? ? ? ? ? ?

26.) Who has not seen God?

27.) He that does _____ is of God.

28.) John said Demetrius was godly because he:
    a) did not like Diotrephes
    b) praised all of John's epistles
    c) was a true Christian witness
    d) gave John fine food and lodgings

29.) John's third epistle is short because he:
    a) was running late because he wasted too much time on computer games
    b) ran out of things to write
    c) ran out of ink
    d) hoped to see them in person soon

30.) What does John wish Gaius in the letter's closing?

A WORD FROM JUDE

Jude

1.) Who wrote the Epistle of Jude?

2.) Did you know that Jude was one of Jesus' brothers?

3.) This letter is written to:
   a) Christians in the early church
   b) Paul the Apostle
   c) Jesus
   d) Elvis Presley

4.) What three things does Jude wish for his readers?

5.) Jude was upset with ungodly men in the church because they:
   a) did not give their full 10% tithe
   b) denied our Lord God and His Son Jesus Christ
   c) sacrificed bulls instead of bullocks
   d) spent all of the church's money on themselves

6.) Jude told his readers to remember two cities that were punished by God. What are the names of the cities?

7.) Jude warns his readers not to be like:
   a) Abel
   b) Cain
   c) Hollywood stars
   d) Moses

8.) Jude says that people who don't love the Lord:
   a) are nice people if you can forget about their unbelief
   b) never loan you any paper if you forget to bring yours to school
   c) copy off of your paper during tests
   d) will say nice things they don't mean to important people who can help them

9.) Name another book of the Bible whose wise sayings warn about flatterers.

10.) What is the last word of Jude's epistle?

11.) People who deny Jesus Christ:
   a) are more interested in worldly things like being rich and popular than in God
   b) will always be famous because they shock people
   c) are true Christians
   d) will go to heaven

12.) How can Christians build themselves up?

13.) Christians should keep themselves:
   a) in church at all times
   b) on every church committee to show God how hard they work
   c) in with the bad crowd at school
   d) in God's love

? ? ? ? ? ? ? ? ?

14.) What does Jesus Christ offer us?

15.) To whom does Jude give praise and
glory?

1.) You can find the story of Noah's ark in the Book of
   a. Genesis
   b. Revelation
   c. The Love Boat
   d. Noah

2.) True or False: In Noah's time, God was pleased with His creation.

3.) In Noah's time, God decided He would

   a. rain manna on all the people.
   b. destroy all the people, animals, and birds He had created.
   c. give everyone a computer for school.
   d. send missionaries to give everyone a New Testament Bible.

4.) True or False: Noah was the only good man living in his time.

5.) How many sons did Noah have?

6.) Can you name Noah's sons? Hint: One of them has the same name as a famous Virginia meat product.

7.) Did you know that God told Noah to take seven pairs of each type of bird with him into the ark? (Genesis 7:3). He also told Noah to take one pair of each ritually unclean animal and seven pairs of each ritually clean animal (Genesis 7:2).

8.) What is a ritually clean beast?

9.) When the flood started Noah was
    a. 6 years old   c. 600 years old
    b. 60 years old   d. 666 years old

10.) How long did it rain?

11.) Did you know that the water rose until it was about twenty-five feet over the highest mountains? (Genesis 7:20).

12.) Noah could see the mountaintops after
    a. 7 1/2 months
    b. 10 months
    c. 7 days
    d. 40 days and 40 nights

13.) Did you know that, after the flood, the water did not start going down for 150 days?

14.) True or False: The first bird Noah sent out from the ark was a dove.

15.) After the second time out, the dove brought Noah
   a. an Amy Grant CD
   b. another dove
   c. a McDonald's Happy Meal
   d. an olive branch

16.) True or False: Noah was 601 years old when he and his family got out of the ark.

17.) After God saved Noah's family from the flood, Noah
   a. opened Noah's Yacht Club
   b. made a golden calf
   c. built an altar to God and made sacrifices upon it
   d. learned to swim

18.) True or False: God promised not to destroy the earth by flood again.

19.) What caused God to make such a promise?

20.) What do we often see after rainfall that reminds us of God's promise to Noah?

A TOWERING PROBLEM

1.) Where in the Bible can you find the story of the Tower of Babel?

2.) True or False: When the people first started building the Tower of Babel, they all spoke the same language.

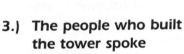

3.) The people who built the tower spoke
   a. Latin
   b. Hebrew
   c. French and Spanish
   d. an unspecified language

4.) Did you know that the Tower of Babel was built in Babylonia? The Bible says the people had settled on a plain in Shinar, which was in ancient Babylonia (Genesis 11:2).

5.) The tower was built of
   a. wood
   b. stone
   c. brick
   d. steel

6.) True or False: The people were building a city as well as a tower.

7.) The people wanted a tower that would
   a. let them see the Atlantic Ocean
   b. be three feet taller than the Empire State Building
   c. make a suitable home for Rapunzel
   d. reach to heaven

8.) True or False: God was happy when He saw the tower.

9.) When He saw the tower, God
   a. gave the people a golden calf
   b. asked Satan to loan the builders
      pitchforks to help them finish it
   c. told the workmen how to make
      better bricks
   d. made the people all speak different
      languages so they couldn't finish
      the work

10.) Why is the story of the
     Tower of Babel important?

GOD'S PROMISE TO ABRAHAM

1.) Did you know that the story of Abraham is found in the book of Genesis?

2.) In which chapter can you find the story of God's promise to Abraham?

3.) True or False: Abraham was named Abram before God changed his name.

4.) How old was Abraham when God appeared to him?

5.) God told Abraham to
   a. build an ark
   b. become Jesus' disciple
   c. obey Him
   d. make a movie called *The Ten Commandments*

6.) When Abraham saw God, he
   a. told God he was afraid
   b. bowed down, touching his face to the ground
   c. built an altar
   d. asked Him for a son

7.) God wanted to make a covenant with Abraham. What is a covenant?

8.) True or False: God promised Abraham he would have many descendants.

9.) A descendant is
   a. a member of a future generation
   b. an ancestor
   c. a person walking down a staircase
   d. an airplane going down in the sky

10.) God also promised Abraham
   a. great riches
   b. a chariot and seven swift horses
   c. a coat of many colors
   d. the land of Canaan

11.) True or False: God plans for His covenant with Abraham to last forever.

12.) God gave Abram the name "Abraham" because
   a. it fit better with the song "Father Abraham"
   b. it was easier to spell
   c. Abraham was to be the father of many nations
   d. He wanted to name him after Abraham Lincoln

13.) True or False: God said that some of Abraham's descendants would be kings.

14.) True or False: As part of the covenant, God wanted Abraham and his descendants to worship Him.

15.) God changed the name of Abraham's wife. Do you remember what Sarah's name was before God changed it?

16.) God promised Sarah she would
   a. never have to work again
   b. live in a tent until she was ninety
   c. have a baby
   d. be the first woman president of the
      United States

17.) When God promised Abraham that
    his wife, Sarah, would have a baby,
    Abraham
   a. bowed down to God
   b. laughed
   c. sang God a psalm
   d. wrote the Pentateuch

18.) Which did God promise Sarah, a baby
    boy or a baby girl?

19.) Abraham was surprised by God's
    promise because Sarah
   a. had vowed never to have children
   b. was CEO of a large company and
      had no time for kids
   c. was ninety years old, which is
      usually too old to have a baby
   d. already had thirteen boys

20.) How old was Abraham when God promised him that Sarah would bear a baby?

21.) Did you know that Abraham suggested another heir? He told God that his son Ishmael could be his heir (Genesis 17:18).

22.) An heir is
   a. a person with too much hair
   b. an honest mistake
   c. a person who receives an inheritance
   d. an airhead

23.) True or False: God agreed with Abraham that Ishmael should be Abraham's heir.

24.) True or False: All males in Abraham's household were required to take a physical mark to show they were in covenant with God.

25.) How do you think Abraham's covenant with God affects you today?

1.) Did you know that the Ten Commandments appear in the Bible twice? You can find them in Exodus 20:1–17 and Deuteronomy 5:1–21.

2.) True or False: Exodus and Deuteronomy are both New Testament books.

3.) Who wrote the first five books of the Bible?

4.) Did you know that the first five books of the Bible are called the Pentateuch?

5.) Can you name all five books of the Pentateuch?

6.) When God issued the Ten Commandments, He was on
a. the banks of the River Jordan
b. Mount Sinai
c. Israel's TV Channel 6
d. Mount Ararat

7.) Did you know that *Exodus* means departure?

8.) When God gave them the Ten Commandments, the Israelites had just
   a. traveled the Information Highway
   b. been brought out of slavery in Egypt
   c. discovered electricity
   d. celebrated the release of the movie *Star Wars*

9.) True or False: The First Commandment is God's law to worship no other god except Him.

10.) Do you think The First Commandment is the most important? Why?

11.) True or False: It is okay to worship statues, money, and other earthly goods as long as we attend church every Sunday.

12.) What does God mean when He says not to take His name "in vain"?

13.) God commands us to set aside one day a week to
   a. gather manna
   b. read the Bible and only drink water all day
   c. watch cartoons
   d. keep holy, cease work, and remember His people's deliverance from Egypt

14.) True or False: On the Sabbath, the head of the household may rest, but everyone else should work.

15.) Why did God say He wanted us to rest every seventh day?

16.) Did you know that the Ten Commandments are divided into two sections? The first four tell us how to show love to God. The rest tell us how to show love to other people.

17.) Think about the Sabbath. How do you show your love to God on His special day?

18.) God tells us to honor our

   a. pastor
   b. friends
   c. father and mother
   d. teachers and principal

19.) True or False: The Sixth Commandment tells us not to murder.

20.) God's commandment not to commit adultery shows us how much God values marriage. Where does God establish the institution of marriage?

21.) The Eighth Commandment tells us not to
   a. burp in public
   b. be mean to our brothers and sisters
   c. steal
   d. be angry with others

22.) The King James Version of the Bible tells us that God says not to "bear false witness" against our neighbor. The New International Version says we should not give "false testimony." What do these phrases in Exodus 20:16 and Deuteronomy 5:20 mean?

23.) Sometimes it is hard not to lie because the truth can hurt someone's feelings. How can you be truthful without being mean?

24.) God tells us not to covet other people's possessions. That means we should not
a. steal from our friends
b. destroy other people's belongings
c. make fun of others
d. wish we had our neighbor's stuff

25.) God also gave Moses other laws. Most of them can be found in the book of
a. Leviticus   c. Acts
b. Numbers   d. Revelation

26.) Did you know that God wrote the Ten Commandments Himself? (Deuteronomy 9:9–11).

27.) The Lord wrote the Ten Commandments on
a. sheepskin   c. parchment
b. stone tablets   d. Thursday

28.) True or False: The original copy of the Ten Commandments is on display at the Jerusalem Museum.

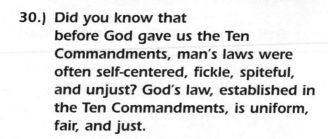

29.) Now that you have learned about The Ten Commandments, can you name all of them?

30.) Did you know that before God gave us the Ten Commandments, man's laws were often self-centered, fickle, spiteful, and unjust? God's law, established in the Ten Commandments, is uniform, fair, and just.

JOSHUA'S FAMOUS BATTLE

1.) Did you know that when he was a young man, Joshua served in the tabernacle? (Exodus 33:11).

2.) True or False: Moses was led by God to appoint Joshua to be his successor.

3.) Did you know that Joshua is the first of the Bible's historical books? Although the first five books discuss history, they are considered part of the Pentateuch.

4.) The book of Joshua begins recording what happened right after
   a. the Israelites went whitewater rafting on the Jordan River
   b. the American Revolution
   c. the death of Moses
   d. the birth of Jesus

5.) Is Joshua found in the Old Testament or the New Testament?

6.) Who wrote the book of Joshua?

7.) God told Joshua to take the people of Israel to the land He had promised them, located across the
a. Red Sea   c. Jordan River
b. Grand Canyon   d. Nile River

8.) True or False: God said the Israelites should never become discouraged because He would be with them wherever they went.

9.) Joshua's spies in Jericho stayed at
a. a Holiday Inn
b. a Pharisee's house
c. the home of a wicked woman
d. Mary Magdalene's house

10.) True or False: Rahab protected the spies from the men of Jericho.

11.) Did you know that no one could leave or enter a city after the gate was closed at sundown? Rahab tricked the men who were chasing

Joshua's spies and told them to look outside the city. Because the men were locked out after sundown, they could not harm the spies (Joshua 2:4–7).

12.) Rahab hid the spies
    a. on the roof.
    b. in the wine cellar.
    c. in the bathtub.
    d. under her bed.

13.) Did you know that in addition to protecting them, Rahab gave the spies valuable information? She told them that the people of Jericho were afraid of the Israelites. This gave the spies confidence that the Lord would help them conquer Jericho (Joshua 2:9 and 2:24).

14.) True or False: Rahab accepted the Lord and asked the spies for mercy.

15.) Why did Rahab protect the spies?

16.) Did you know that God stopped the Jordan River from flowing while the Israelites crossed it into the Promised Land? The river was usually flooded at that time of year, so crossing it on foot would have been impossible without God's miracle. The stopping of the river also allowed the ark of the covenant to stay dry while the priests carried it (Joshua 3:14–17).

17.) What was the ark of the covenant?

18.) How many men crossed the plains of Jericho to fight for the Lord?

19.) The Israelites no longer had manna to eat after they had
   a. been punished for watching too much TV.
   b. eaten food grown in the Promised Land.
   c. gotten tired of eating quail meat.
   d. sinned.

20.) What was manna?

21. Did you know that God sent a divine commander to help the Israelites defeat Jericho? Although the Bible calls him a man, we know he was divine, because Joshua bowed before him and the man told Joshua to take off his shoes because he was on holy ground (Joshua 5:13–15).

22. True or False: The walls of Jericho came tumbling down after the Israelites threw rocks and stones at them.

23. Whose family was spared during the fall of Jericho?

24. All the silver, gold, bronze, and iron in Jericho was
    a. used to improve the ark of the covenant.
    b. put into the Lord's treasury.
    c. used to build the Tower of Babel.
    d. made into fancy jewelry.

25. True or False: After the fall of Jericho, Joshua became famous in the land.

DAVID FIGHTS GOLIATH

1.) You can find the story of David's battle with Goliath in
   a. 1 Samuel
   b. the Book of David
   c. the book *Goliath: The Bigger They Are, The Harder They Fall*
   d. Jude

2.) Did you know that Goliath of Gath was over nine feet tall? (1 Samuel 17:4).

3.) True or False: Goliath was never heavily armed. He depended on his size to protect him.

4.) True or False: When Goliath challenged the Israelites to send a man to fight him, many men eagerly volunteered.

5.) Why did David visit the Israelites' battlefield?

6.) Before he met Goliath, David
   a. was next in line to be a high priest
   b. tended sheep
   c. was a prince of Israel
   d. learned to fight giants by jousting with a cousin

7.) Gath was located in what country? Hint: Goliath was from Gath and the Israelites were battling his country.

8.) True or False: While David was visiting his brothers on the battlefield, Goliath challenged the Israelites.

9.) Did you know that King Saul had promised a reward to the person who killed Goliath? In addition to money, King Saul promised his daughter in marriage, and the victor's father's family would not have to pay taxes (1 Samuel 17:25).

10.) True or False: David's brothers were sure David could easily slay Goliath.

11.) When David heard the giant's challenge, he
   a. wondered how Goliath dared to defy the army of the living God
   b. became scared and ran home
   c. decided to videotape Goliath to show on *Real TV*
   d. threatened to take Goliath to court for saying mean things

12.) Saul did not want David to fight Goliath because David
   a. already had plans to attend seminary
   b. was a consultant to King Saul on how to fix Social Security
   c. was only a boy
   d. was an old man

13.) Did you know that King Saul gave David his own bronze helmet and coat of armor to use when fighting Goliath? (1 Samuel 17:38).

14.) True or False: David convinced King Saul to let him fight Goliath by telling him that God had protected David from the lions and bears that attacked his sheep.

15.) David took Saul's armor off, because
   a. the color bronze clashed with his dark hair
   b. Saul's armor was out of style
   c. he couldn't walk in it because he wasn't used to such cumbersome armor
   d. his friends at the mall would make fun of him for not looking cool

16.) How many smooth stones did David pick up to battle Goliath?

17.) True or False: When Goliath saw David coming to battle him, he shook with fear.

18.) David told Goliath that his victory
over him would prove that
a. the pen is mightier than the sword
b. he had been paying attention
when he watched *Terminator 2*
c. size means nothing
d. there is a God in Israel

19.) True or False: Goliath fell with the
first stone David hurled at him.

20.) After Goliath died, the Israelites
a. chased the Philistines back to their
own country
b. offered the Philistines a permanent
peace treaty
c. slept
d. sang "I'm in the Lord's Army!"

ELISHA PERFORMS MANY MIRACLES

1.) True or False: Elisha was the son of the prophet Elijah.

2.) You can find out about Elisha in
a. 1 Kings
b. 2 Kings
c. Matthew
d. Revelation

3.) Did you know that Elijah was taken to heaven by a chariot of fire? (1Kings 2:11).

4.) Can you name another godly person who was taken to heaven without dying?

5.) True or False: Elisha asked for a "double portion" of Elijah's spirit.

6.) Elisha's first miracle was
   a. making 5,000 Spamburgers from one can of Spam
   b. dividing the Jordan River and walking on dry land
   c. inventing the cotton gin
   d. getting the children of Jericho to eat broccoli soup

7.) True or False: The fifty prophets of Jericho saw the miracle and proclaimed that Elijah's power was upon Elisha.

8.) In Jericho, Elisha
   a. opened a Coca Cola factory
   b. gave a bowl of broccoli soup to every child he met
   c. made the water pure
   d. turned water into wine

9.) Some boys in Bethel made fun of Elisha for being
   a. a stamp collector
   b. vertically challenged
   c. bald
   d. a dweeb

10.) Did you know that Elisha was so famous, kings asked him for advice? King Jehoshaphat of Judah, King Joram of Israel, and the King of Edom asked him how to defeat the Moabites (2 Kings 3:13).

11.) The Moabites had
a. poisoned the Jordan River
b. turned the Nile River red
c. rebelled against Israel
d. been involved in a junk-bond scandal on Wall Street

12.) True or False: Elisha told the kings to build ditches in a dry stream bed.

13.) The next day, the Moabites decided to loot the Israelites' camp because
a. Elisha told them to
b. Jezebel rose from the dead and promised victory
c. they thought the water they saw around the camp was blood
d. they had promised to bring their girlfriends some jewelry

14.) What happened when the Moabites reached the Israelites' camp?

15.) True or False: The Israelites conquered all of Moab until only the capital city of Kir-haraseth was left.

16.) Later, a widow asked Elisha for help because she
a. was in debt
b. wanted to be beautiful
c. wanted to find another husband
d. wanted him to change the school cafeteria menu from fish sticks to pizza

17.) The only item the widow had in her house was
a. a small coin called a mite
b. a brass monkey
c. a picture of Jesus
d. a small jar of olive oil

18.) Describe the miracle that happened when the widow followed Elisha's instructions.

19.) True or False: Because of Elisha's advice, the widow had enough money to pay off her debts, with enough left over to live on.

20.) Elisha offered to put in a good word with the king for a rich woman who had been kind to him. Did she accept his offer?

21.) Elisha rewarded the Shunammite woman's kindness by
   a. praising her to the king
   b. promising her that she would have a baby
   c. giving her permission to charge toll to people entering Jerusalem
   d. giving her free cable television for a year

22.) The kindness that the woman had done for Elisha was
   a. giving him water at the well
   b. buying him tickets to see WrestleFest America
   c. setting up a room for him to stay in when he visited
   d. washing his feet with expensive CK One perfume

23.) True or False: Years later, Elisha performed a miracle for the woman's son.

24.) Elisha:
   a. brought the boy back from the dead
   b. refused to perform a miracle
   c. healed the boy's blindness
   d. gave the boy wisdom so he could pass his college entrance exams

25.) Did you know that Elisha fed 100 men with twenty loaves of bread? Even though this normally would not have been enough food for so many, they all feasted and had food left over (2 Kings 4:42–44).

26.) Which one of Jesus' miracles does this story make you remember?

27.) True or False: Elisha purified a pot of stew that contained poisonous gourds.

28.) True or False: Naaman was a respected Egyptian commander.

29.) Naaman suffered from
- a. leprosy
- b. the flu
- c. negative cash flow
- d. cowardice

30.) Who suggested that Elisha could cure Naaman?

31.) Did you know that when Naaman arrived in Israel to see Elisha, he had a letter from his king, thirty thousand pieces of silver, six thousand pieces of gold, and ten changes of fine clothes? (2 Kings 5:5–6).

32.) When King Jehoram of Israel saw Naaman, he thought
- a. *I'll be rich now!*
- b. *I will only ask for the silver, lest I look greedy*
- c. *I do not have the power of God! The Syrian king wants to quarrel with me*
- d. *Gross! A leper!*

33.) True or False: Elisha was not afraid to try to heal Naaman. He told the king that he would prove Israel had a prophet.

34.) Elisha sent his servant to tell Naaman to
   a. wash seven times in the Jordan River
   b. sacrifice five rams
   c. sit on a stump and say, "Bobiddy Boo Boo!" three times
   d. go to a leper colony

35.) When Naaman was told what he should do to get well, he
   a. cried   c. was eager to proceed
   b. was angry   d. decided to kill Elisha

36.) True or False: Elisha's instructions caused Naaman to become even more sick.

37.) After Naaman was cured, whose god did he vow to worship?

38.) Did you know that Naaman asked Elisha for some of Israel's soil to take back with him to Syria? (2 Kings 5:17). At this time, people believed you could only worship a god on his own land. Today, we know the Lord can be worshipped anywhere.

39.) The amount of soil Naaman took with
   him was
   a. a jar full   c. a peck
   b. a bushel   d. two mule loads

40.) Did you know Elisha refused to accept
   any payment in return for curing
   Naaman? (2 Kings 5:16).

41.) True or False: Elisha's servant ran after
   Naaman and asked him for money and
   clothes.

42.) Did Naaman give the servant any
   gifts?

43.) True or False: Elisha was happy with
   the servant's actions.

44.) When he heard what Gehazi had
   done, Elisha
   a. rewarded him with half the money
   b. complimented Gehazi on how smart
      he was
   c. gave him a bigger Christmas bonus
      than usual for his efforts
   d. said that Gehazi and his family
      would always be plagued with
      leprosy

A VISIT FROM THE QUEEN

1.) Can you find the story of the queen's visit to Solomon in the Old Testament or the New Testament?

2.) The queen was from
   a. Egypt
   b. France
   c. Babylon
   d. Sheba

3.) The queen visited King Solomon because
   a. she had heard of his fame.
   b. she was looking for a husband.
   c. she was hungry and heard he served great food.
   d. he had the best pinball arcade in all of Israel.

4.) Did you know that the queen's visit is recorded in two places in the Bible? You can read about it in 1 Kings 10:1–13 and 2 Chronicles 9:1–12.

5.) Did you know that, according to Bible scholars, the queen's country was located about twelve hundred miles from Jerusalem? Although airplanes make traveling such distances easy today, the queen had to go by camel or horseback, making the trip long and difficult.

6.) True or False: The queen wanted to test Solomon with difficult questions.

7.) The queen's first question was
   a. Which came first, the chicken or the egg?
   b. Where is your mine, King Solomon?
   c. Is the moon made of cheese?
   d. unknown. Her questions are not recorded in the Bible.

8.) The queen was amazed by Solomon's
   a. wisdom and sacrifices to God
   b. hairstyle
   c. ability to recite the entire Bible from memory
   d. skill at Nintendo

9.) The queen was also amazed by Solomon's
   a. willingness to live a life of poverty
   b. allegiance to Jesus Christ
   c. riches, palace, food, and servants
   d. ability to read her mind and perform magic tricks

10.) True or False: The queen told Solomon she was disappointed that he didn't know as much as she had been told.

11.) True or False: After she had spoken with Solomon, the queen praised the Lord.

12.) If the queen did praise God, why would this be important?

13.) Did you know that the queen gave Solomon 666 talents of gold, and many spices and jewels? (1 Kings 10:9 and 2 Chronicles 9:10).

14.) If one talent weighs seventy-five pounds, how many pounds of gold did the Queen of Sheba give to Solomon?

NEHEMIAH BUILDS A WALL

1.) Can you find the book of Nehemiah in the Old Testament or the New Testament?

2.) Who wrote the book of Nehemiah?

3.) Did you know that the book of Nehemiah was written about 430 BC?

4.) In Nehemiah's time, the Jews in Jerusalem were
   a. rich
   b. happy
   c. suffering
   d. in charge of Jerusalem's stock exchange

5.) True or False: When the book of Nehemiah begins, the walls of Jerusalem have just been built.

6.) True or False: Nehemiah asked the Lord to allow the king to have mercy on him.

7.) When he heard about the people's plight, Nehemiah
a. wept and prayed to God
b. ran away to Tarsus
c. recommended psychotherapy
d. fled and ended up in the belly of a fish

8.) Nehemiah was the king's
a. food taster
b. cup bearer
c. jester
d. spin doctor

9.) King Artaxerxes noticed that Nehemiah
a. had spilled wine on the palace's \ carpet
b. looked sad
c. had the ability to interpret dreams
d. had written him a message on the wall

10.) Nehemiah asked the king if he could
  a. give the Israelites straw to help
     them make better bricks
  b. start a program called *The Great
     Society* to help the Jews in exile
  c. go back and rebuild the city of
     Jerusalem
  d. grant the Jews more time off from
     work

11.) Did the king grant Nehemiah's request?

12.) True or False: Nehemiah told the king
he was sad about Jerusalem.

13.) Did you know that travel to Judah would
have placed Nehemiah in great danger?
Nehemiah needed letters from the king
giving him permission to pass through
enemy territory. The king also sent along
soldiers to protect Nehemiah from harm
(Nehemiah 2:7–9).

14.) The animal Nehemiah took with him was
  a. his pet goldfish
  b. his donkey
  c. a camel with bad breath
  d. a pet boa constrictor to squeeze his
     opponents to death

15.) True or False: Rebuilding Jerusalem was risky because it was against the emperor's wishes.

16.) Who was Nehemiah counting on for his success?

17.) Did you know that King David was buried in Jerusalem? (Nehemiah 3:16).

18.) The wall was built in a circle, starting and finishing at
a. Pizza Hut of Jerusalem
b. David's tomb
c. a statue of Hermes
d. the sheep gate

19.) True or False: Everyone was happy to see the new wall being built.

20.) True or False: When Nehemiah realized that people were making fun of his efforts to rebuild the wall, he called off the project and went back to Persia.

21.) Did you know that half the men had to stand guard, armed with spears, while the other half built the wall? This slowed down their work but protected them against opposition to the project (Nehemiah 4:21).

22.) Later, Jerusalem's Jews complained that
   a. they were too poor to feed their families
   b. they had gotten tired manna
   c. there was a shortage Andy Griffith CDs
   d. the wall should be pai gold

23.) Nehemiah was angry when he discovered
   a. the leaders had been keeping all the gold paint for themselves
   b. the paint store wouldn't refund his money
   c. the rich Jews were taking advantage of their poor relatives
   d. he wouldn't be paid the thirty silver talents he had been promised

24.) True or False: The leaders promised to return everyone's property and not try to collect any debts.

25.) Did you know that when Nehemiah was governor of Judah, he fed a big crowd of more than one hundred people every day? His menu included one beef, six fine sheep, and many chickens (Nehemiah 5:17–18).

26.) To show how God would punish any leader who didn't keep his promise to help the poor, Nehemiah
a. shook his fist
b. shook his sash
c. invented a dance called the "Hippy Hippy Shake"
d. told the people how to make milkshakes

27.) Did the leaders keep their promise to help the poor?

28.) True or False: Nehemiah took advantage of all the privileges he was entitled to as governor of Judah.

29.) Why didn't Nehemiah claim his big allowance?

30.) How many days did it take to build the entire wall?

LAMENTATIONS

1.) Where in the Bible can you find the book of Lamentations?

2.) *Lamenting* means
   a. being sorry about something
   b. being glad about something
   c. arguing
   d. singing

3.) Did you know that the prophet Jeremiah wrote Lamentations?

4.) In this book, Jeremiah laments
   a. the cancellation of God's promise to provide manna to the people
   b. the death of Moses
   c. having to eat spinach lasagna
   d. the destruction of Jerusalem in 586 BC

5.) Did you know that the book of Lamentations consists of five poems?

6.) True or False: The first poem is about Jerusalem's sorrow.

7.) The second poem speaks of God's
   a. love   c. mercy
   b. anger   d. kindness

8.) True or False: Although God punished Jerusalem, He brought the Jews back to Himself.

9.) True or False: The fifth poem is a prayer for mercy.

10.) Think about the last time you asked God for forgiveness. How did you feel? Did you know it is important to ask God for forgiveness when you do wrong?

1.) Did you know that the prophet Hosea preached around 721 BC?

2.) What was the name of Hosea's wife?

3.) God told Hosea to name his son _____ because he would destroy Israel's military power in the valley of _____.

4.) Did you know that Hosea's children's names symbolized God's coming punishment for Israel? As you read the Bible, notice how often names were given that had special meanings.

5.) Hosea's first daughter was named Lo-Ruhamah, meaning "unloved," because God would no longer show love to the _____.

6.) True or False: God told Hosea to name his second son Lo-Ammi, meaning "not my people," because the people of Israel were not His people and He was not their God.

7.) Was God planning to be angry with Israel forever?

8.) True or False: Gomer was a good wife to Hosea.

9.) Hosea planned to
   a. have twelve children with Gomer
   b. be unfaithful to Gomer for revenge
   c. win Gomer back
   d. give Gomer the latest computer for her birthday

10.) How was Gomer's unfaithfulness to Hosea like Israel's unfaithfulness to God?

11.) What will happen when Israel returns to God?

12.) True or False: God looked kindly upon the Israelite priests during this time.

13.) God was upset with the people of Israel for
   a. eating unclean food
   b. worshipping other gods
   c. starting a contemporary church service
   d. playing Christian rock instead of old hymns

14.) God was angry at another country besides Israel. Can you name it?

15.) God is angry with the other country for
   a. invading and oppressing Israel
   b. worshipping false gods
   c. helping Israel
   d. eating unclean food

16.) True or False: God says perhaps
Israel will look for Him in her
suffering.

17.) What does God say He wants from
His people?

18.) The Lord says the people of Israel are
like a
a. wayward servant
b. stubborn mule
c. bagel with cream cheese
d. half-baked loaf of bread

19.) What type of bird does God say the
nation of Israel is like?

20.) When God compared Israel to this
bird, He meant Israel was
a. strong and true
b. soaring upward
c. soft and feathery
d. flitting from place to place

21.) Did you know that one false god the Israelites worshipped was Baal? Hosea says the Israelites gave Baal corn, wine, oil, and money (Hosea 2:8). The Lord was not pleased when they gave His gifts to a false god.

22.) True or False: God said Israel will be punished for her sins.

23.) Hosea said that the Israelites would return to Egypt. Why would this be a punishment for them?

24.) The false idols the Israelites worshipped were shaped like
   a. Goliath's shield   c. ravens
   b. calves   d. a cedar tree

25.) True or False: Hosea asked the Israelites to return to God.

26.) Hosea asked God to
   a. punish the Israelites greatly
   b. send a plague to the land
   c. send them into slavery
   d. forgive their sins

27.) Hosea asked the Israelites to offer God a prayer (Hosea 14:2). Think about your prayers to God. Do you just ask Him to do things for you? Or do you thank Him for all He has done for you?

28.) What do the people promise in their prayer?

29.) The Lord promise
   a. a new life
   b. a new healthca
   c. that their chil-
      dren will never
      have to go
      to school
   d. that they
      will never have
      to eat spinach

30.) Did you know that even though God punished Israel, He loved them all the same? He loves us, too. John 3:16 tells us just how much. Can you say John 3:16 from memory?

JOEL

1.) Did you know that the book of Joel makes no mention of any king or foreign nation? This means it is hard for Bible scholars to tell exactly when it was written. However, they believe it was written in the eighth or ninth century, BC.

2.) Who wrote the book of Joel?

3.) You can find the book of Joel in
   a. the Old Testament, after Hosea
   b. the New Testament, before Matthew
   c. the Old Testament, after Daniel
   d. your Bible's concordance

4.) Joel was a
   a. Levite
   b. prophet
   c. tax collector
   d. Hollywood director

5.) True or False: A prophet tells what God plans to do in the future.

6.) Joel talked about a time in the past when the land was filled with
a. milk and honey   c. floods
b. locusts   d. thieves

7.) True or False: The people were upset because their crops had been destroyed by bugs.

8.) The Lord wanted the people to
a. invite Him to the Super Bowl
b. repent of their sins
c. stop eating fruit from the Garden of Eden
d. build an ark

9.) True or False: God restored Israel's fertile land.

10.) True or False: God told the land and animals not to be afraid.

11.) Why should the people be glad?

12.) True or False: God will judge the nations in the Land Before Time.

13.) Did you know that the term *Valley of Jehoshaphat* means "Yahweh judges"? Today's English Version of the Bible translates Valley of Jehoshaphat as "Valley of Judgment."

14.) Egypt and Edom will be punished for attacking
    a. The United States
    b. Saudi Arabia
    c. Jordan
    d. Judah

15.) Where will the Lord live when He returns to Earth?

1.) Did you know that the prophet Micah was from Judah? He was afraid his country would be punished by God. He wanted to warn them to repent (Micah 1:9).

2.) Who wrote the book of Micah?

3.) You can find the book of Micah in
   a. the Old Testament, after the book of Jonah
   b. the Old Testament, before the book of Genesis
   c. the New Testament, after the book of Revelation
   d. the index of the Bible

4.) True or False: Idolatry is the worship of false gods.

5.) The country of Judah was guilty of
   a. watching too much TV
   b. idolatry
   c. laziness
   d. being late for school too often

6.) What did Micah say about Samaria?

7.) Micah said he would show his sorrow about God's punishment by
   a. writing a Top 40 country western song
   b. giving more money to the church treasury
   c. eating locusts and wild honey
   d. walking naked and howling

8.) True or False: Micah said Judah would not be punished.

9.) The people did not like Micah's prophecy (Micah 2:6). Why?

10.) Micah said the people wanted a prophet who would
   a. lie   c. steal
   b. cheat   d. sing

11.) True or False: Micah had nothing but good things to say about the rulers of Israel.

12.) Did you know that a part of Micah's prophecy is just like Isaiah's? Micah said the mountain where the temple stands will be the highest of all, attracting many people. (Compare Micah 4:1–4 and Isaiah 2:2–4.)

13.) True or False: In Micah 4:1–4 and Isaiah 2:2–4 God promises peace. Hint: You may want to read question 12 again while you think about this.

14.) Did you know that some prophets took money in exchange for telling people what they wanted to hear instead of the truth? God was very upset with these false prophets (Micah 3:11).

15.) The false prophets thought it was all right to lie because
   a. they thought the Lord was with them
   b. their daughters were beautiful
   c. they knew they could get away with it
   d. they were rich

16.) True or False: Micah says that even though Israel will be punished, the country will once again worship the Lord.

17.) God promises Israel a ruler out of Bethlehem whose family line can be traced to ancient times. Who do you think this ruler is?

18.) True or False: Bethlehem was one of the great cities of Micah's time.

19.) The Bible in Today's English Version says: "When he comes, he will rule his people with the strength that comes from the Lord and with the majesty of the Lord God himself. His people will live in safety because people all over the earth will acknowledge his greatness, and he will bring peace" (Micah 5:4–5).

In this passage, Micah is talking about Jesus. Think about the power and glory of Jesus.

20.) Micah prophesied that Israel would conquer
a. Assyria   c. Egypt
b. France   d. the world

21.) True or False: God wants animal sacrifices from Christians.

22.) True or False: Evil people who get their treasures dishonestly will enjoy them.

23.) Read Micah 18–20. This passage is read in Jewish synagogues on the Day of Atonement.

24.) Did you know that the Lord said the evil people of Micah's time followed King Omri's and King Ahab's wicked ways? (Micah 6:16). This means we should follow the Lord's ways over any earthly ruler's.

1.) How many Gospels are there in the Bible?

2.) In your Bible, you can find the Gospels in
   a. the first part of the New Testament
   b. the first part of the Old Testament
   c. the concordance
   d. the last part of the New Testament

3.) What is a concordance?

4.) The Gospels are the books of
   a. Genesis, Exodus, Leviticus, Numbers, and Deuteronomy
   b. Jude and Revelation
   c. Matthew, Mark, Luke, and John
   d. Genesis and Matthew

5.) All four Gospels tell us about
   a. the life and ministry of Jesus
   b. Paul's life
   c. the events surrounding Joshua's prophecies
   d. how to get good grades without doing any work

6.) Your Bible may have red letters in some places. What do they mean?

7.) If your Bible has red letters, you can see them in the Gospels and in
   a. Genesis
   b. the Acts of the Apostles and Revelation
   c. no other book of the Bible
   d. Psalms

8.) True or False: Jesus wrote parts of all four Gospels.

9.) Did you know that Matthew was also called Levi? (Mark 2:14).

10.) Matthew
  a. was the disciple who betrayed Jesus
  b. collected taxes for Rome
  c. ran the waterslide at the King's Dominion amusement park in Israel
  d. was a Roman soldier

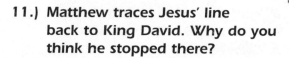

11.) Matthew traces Jesus' line back to King David. Why do you think he stopped there?

12.) Did you know that the Gospel of Mark is the shortest Gospel?

13.) True or False: Luke is the longest Gospel.

14.) Which Gospel has the most chapters?

15.) Did you know that John was one of the disciples in Jesus' inner circle?

THE BIRTH OF JESUS

1.) True or False: The story of Jesus' birth is found in the book of Matthew.

2.) Did you know there were fourteen generations from Abraham to David, fourteen from David to the exile in Babylon, and fourteen from then to Jesus' birth? (Matthew 1:17).

3.) When she discovered she would give birth to Jesus, Mary was engaged to
   a. Adam   c. Moses
   b. Joseph   d. Lot

4.) Did you know that Mary's fiancé was a descendant of King David? (Luke 1:27).

5.) Who first told Mary she would have a baby?

6.) True or False: Mary visited her cousin Elizabeth in Judea after she discovered she would give birth to God's son.

7.) True or False: In a dream, an angel told Joseph he should not be afraid to take Mary as his wife.

8.) Did you know that Jesus was born in the same town as King David? (Luke 2:4)

9.) In which town was Jesus born?

10.) Joseph and Mary went to Bethlehem before Jesus was born because
a. they were on vacation
b. a census was being taken
c. they won a minivan in a sweepstakes and had to go there to claim it
d. Joseph had been offered a job as an innkeeper

11.) True or False: King Herod was filled with joy when he was told the news of Jesus' birth.

12.) Did you know King Herod told the wise men he wanted to worship Jesus? (Matthew 2:8)

13.) The wise men brought Jesus gifts of
    a. gold, frankincense, and myrrh
    b. pearls, rings, and baby rattles.
    c. diapers, formula, and mohair blankets
    d. earrings, spices, and a New Testament Bible

14.) True or False: When Mary and Joseph arrived in town, they stayed at the best hotel.

15.) The shepherds learned about Jesus' birth from
    a. a talking wolf
    b. an invitation they received to His baby shower
    c. angels
    d. Mary

16.) Did you know Luke traced Jesus' ancestors all the way back to Adam? You can find the record of Jesus' lineage in Luke 3:23–38.

17.) True or False: The wise men told King Herod where Jesus was.

18.) True or False: Mary selected Jesus' name herself.

19.) After Jesus was born, an angel told Joseph in a dream to take his family to
   a. Egypt   c. China
   b. Sodom   d. the North Pole

20.) Joseph, Mary, and Jesus stayed in Egypt until Herod
   a. offered Joseph a job at the palace paying 5,000 talents a year
   b. repented of his sins
   c. promised not to kill Jesus
   d. died

21.) Did you know that Joseph was first told in a dream to go to Israel after Herod's death? In a second dream, he was told to go to Galilee. The family settled there in the town of Nazareth (Matthew 2:22).

22.) Jesus was called a _____ because he grew up in Nazareth.

23.) Did you know that when Joseph and Mary presented the baby Jesus to the Lord, they sacrificed a pair of doves and two young pigeons? (Luke 2:24).

24.) Mary and Joseph offered the sacrifice because
    a. it signified their love for each other
    b. they could not find a young ram to sacrifice
    c. it was required by Mosaic Law
    d. they had no silver for the treasury

25.) What godly man was told he would not die before he saw the Messiah?

26.) Jesus was presented to the Lord at the temple in
    a. Nazareth   c. Bethlehem
    b. Jerusalem   d. Egypt

27.) True or False: When the baby Jesus was presented at the temple, two people said that Jesus was the Messiah.

1.) Did you know that Luke is the only Gospel writer who tells us about Jesus' childhood? You can find the story in Luke 2:39–52.

2.) True or False: The books of the Bible that tell us about Jesus' life and ministry are called the Gospels.

3.) Jesus grew up in the town of
   a. Bethlehem   c. Paris
   b. Cairo   d. Nazareth

4.) Jesus' parents went to Jerusalem every year to celebrate the
   a. birth of Jesus   c. Passover
   b. Last Supper   d. Super Bowl

5.) After their trip to Jerusalem when Jesus was twelve, His parents discovered He was not with their group returning to their home in Nazareth. They went back to Jerusalem to look for Him. How long did it take them to find Him?

6.) Joseph and Mary found Jesus

   a. in the Temple, amazing the teachers with His wisdom

   b. at the home of a relative

   c. in a small house with a sign that read "Lost and Found"

   d. eating ice cream at a police station

7.) True or False: Jesus was surprised that Mary and Joseph did not know He would be in the temple.

8.) One man who was important in Jesus' earthly life was

   a. John the Baptist

   b. John the Methodist

   c. John the Presbyterian

   d. John the Lutheran

9.) Did you know that when John the Baptist was born, his father planned to name him Zechariah? The Holy Spirit led his parents to name him John instead (Luke 1:59-63).

10.) John the Baptist ate
   a. granola bars and yogurt
   b. tree bark and wild honey
   c. fried bees and chocolate-covered ants
   d. locusts and wild honey

11.) True or False: John the Baptist preached about Jesus.

12.) True or False: John the Baptist said Jesus would baptize with the Holy Spirit.

13.) When John the Baptist preached about King Herod, he said that Herod
a. was a fine king, worthy of worship
b. had kept his promise to give every student a computer
c. was evil
d. had paid John to say good things about him

14.) What happened to John the Baptist after he preached about King Herod Antipas?

15.) Who baptized Jesus?

16.) After Jesus was baptized, the Holy Spirit came upon Him in the form of
a. a raven
b. an angel
c. a locust
d. a dove

17.) True or False: Jesus turned stones into bread to show the devil He was God's Son.

18.) Satan tempted Jesus by asking Him to turn stones into bread because
   a. Satan's bread had burned in the flames of hell
   b. Jesus' bread would be far better than any bread Satan could make
   c. Jesus was very hungry and wanted to eat because He had not eaten for forty days
   d. Satan's bread tasted like brimstone

19.) Did you know that after Jesus was baptized, the Holy Spirit led Jesus to be tempted by Satan? (Matthew 4:1). Although everyone has a chance to do wrong, God gives us the strength to do what is right.

20.) Satan told Jesus that if He was the Son of God, He ought to be able to safely jump from the top of the Temple and also turn stones into bread. Do you think these were tests of Jesus' pride? Why or why not?

21.) True or False: When Satan told Jesus to jump from the top of the Temple, Jesus told him that we are not to test God.

22.) If Jesus would worship Satan, Satan promised to give Jesus
   a. all the world's kingdoms
   b. bags of gold
   c. heaven's gates
   d. the love of a beautiful woman

23.) Who helped Jesus after He was tempted by Satan?

24.) Did you know that Jesus was about thirty years old when He began His ministry? (Luke 3:23).

25.) Where did Jesus begin His ministry?

JESUS HEALS THE SICK

1.) The Bible tells us about Jesus healing
   sick people in
   a. the Gospels
   b. the Old Testament
   c. Revelation
   d. the *Book of Restoration*

2.) Did you know that the first story
   about Jesus healing someone is in
   Matthew 8:1–4?

3.) True or False: After He healed the sick
   man, Jesus commanded him to tell
   everyone that Jesus was the Messiah.

4.) Jesus healed the Roman officer's
   servant by
   a. touching his cloak
   b. giving him a special medicine
   c. prescribing aspirin and fruit juice
   d. giving an order for him to be
      healed

5.) Did you know that Jesus praised the Roman officer for having great faith? (Matthew 8:10–13).

6.) Whose mother-in-law did Jesus heal of a fever?

7.) Jesus healed the woman's fever by
   a. touching her forehead
   b. touching her hand
   c. giving her two aspirin and advising her to call Him in the morning
   d. telling her to bury a potato under a maple tree at midnight

8.) Did you know that after Jesus cured the woman's fever, He healed many others to fulfill a prophecy of Isaiah? (Matthew 8:16-17).

9.) True or False: When Jesus drove demons from people, the demons proclaimed that Jesus was God's Son.

10.) True or False: Jesus healed the sick because He wanted everyone to know He was the Messiah.

11.) Jesus drove a mob of
demons into a
a. herd of pigs
b. school of fish
c. horde of evil
people
d. rock group

12.) When the local people
found out that Jesus had driven
the mob of demons out of a man,
they
a. feasted for a week
b. were afraid
c. composed a song in His honor
d. made Jesus the town's mayor

13.) True or False: After Jesus drove out
the demons, the people asked Him to
leave their territory.

14.) What did the demon-possessed man
want to do after Jesus healed him?

15.) True or False: Jesus told the man to go back to his family and to tell everyone what God had done for him.

16.) Did the man obey Jesus?

17.) To get well from an illness she had suffered from for twelve years, a woman touched Jesus'
a. cloak   c. feet
b. cup   d. hand

18.) Jesus said the woman had been cured by her
a. money   c. courage
b. beauty   d. faith

19.) Did you know that when the woman was healed, Jesus was on His way to an official's house to heal a little girl?

20.) True or False: When Jesus arrived at the official's house, the little girl had already died.

21.) Jesus said that the child was not dead, but only _____.

22.) Right after Jesus brought the little girl back to life, He healed
a. a little boy who had only two fish and a loaf of bread for lunch
b. two blind men
c. three blind mice
d. ten lepers

23.) What did Jesus tell the people He healed?

24.) Did the people obey Jesus?

25.) Did you know that after Jesus healed a man who could not speak, the Pharisees said Jesus' power came from the leader of demons? (Matthew 9:34). This is a very evil thing to say, because Jesus' power comes from God.

LUKE TELLS US ABOUT JESUS

1.) Where is Luke's Gospel located in the Bible?

2.) Did you know that Luke wrote the Acts of the Apostles?

3.) Where can you find the Acts of the Apostles in the Bible?

4.) True or False: Luke is the only Gospel writer to tell us anything about Jesus' boyhood.

5.) Can you name all four Gospels?

6.) True or False: Jesus healed many people during His ministry on Earth.

7.) Some important people were mad at Jesus because He ate with
a. tax collectors and outcasts
b. no one—He ate alone
c. His family instead of them
d. His favorite disciples

8.) True or False: Jesus showed us it is all right to prepare food on the Sabbath.

9.) To show it is all right to take care of sick people on the Sabbath, Jesus healed
   a. a man with a soccer injury
   b. schoolchildren of chicken pox
   c. a man with a paralyzed hand
   d. a computer with a virus

10.) True or False: When His enemies saw Jesus healing on the Sabbath, they were happy.

11.) A disciple is a
   a. follower
   b. teacher of false doctrine
   c. wife of an epistle
   d. person in charge of computer disks

12.) Jesus chose twelve disciples. How many of them can you name?

13.) Which famous sermon did Jesus preach soon after He chose His disciples?

14.) True or False: Jesus said we should hate our enemies.

15.) Think about a time when someone was mean to you. How did you feel? Was it easy to love and forgive that person?

16.) The King James Version of the Bible quotes Jesus as saying, "And as ye would that men should do to you, do ye also to them" (Luke 6:31). This is called the Golden Rule.  What is the meaning of the Golden Rule?

17.) True or False: When you see someone who is wrong, you should tell that person right away without worrying about your own faults.

18.) While Jesus was visiting Simon the Pharisee, a sinful woman
   a. washed His feet with her tears
   b. tempted Him
   c. danced for Him
   d. peeled grapes and fed them to Him

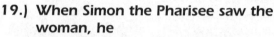

19.) When Simon the Pharisee saw the woman, he
   a. clapped for her
   b. invited her to eat with them
   c. asked her to marry him
   d. said that Jesus shouldn't let a sinful woman touch Him

20.) True or False: Although the woman was sinful, she was trying to show Jesus how much she loved Him.

21.) What did Jesus say to the woman after her visit?

22.) True or False: Jesus had no followers who were women.

LUKE TELLS US
WHAT JESUS SAID

1.) What is a parable?

2.) Jesus told many lessons in parables
   because
   a. He enjoyed confusing everyone
      just for sport
   b. He knew just how to spin a yarn
   c. everyone understood right away
   d. His disciples could understand
      them, but not everyone else

3.) True or False: Jesus revered His
   mother, Mary, over everyone else.

4.) When Jesus performed miracles, some
   people thought He was the resurrected
   a. John the Baptist   c. Paul
   b. Moses   d. Lot

5.) What does the word *resurrected*
   mean?

6.) True or False: Jesus predicted His own death and resurrection.

7.) Jesus said that, to follow Him, you must forget yourself and put Him first (Luke 9:23). How do you do this in your own life?

8.) Did you know that once when Jesus was praying, His face glowed and His clothes became dazzling white? This is called the Transfiguration (Luke 9:29).

9.) During the Transfiguration, Jesus was visited by
a. Noah
b. the three wise men
c. John the Baptist
d. Moses and Elijah

10.) What did Jesus' visitors talk to Him about?

11.) Did you know that after Jesus was visited during the Transfiguration, God's voice came from a cloud. God said, "This is my beloved Son; hear him" (Luke 9:35).

12.) The disciples who saw the transfiguration and heard God's voice

   a. rejoiced and told
      everyone right
      away
   b. were afraid and
      told no one
   c. telephoned
      Eyewitness News
   d. posted pictures
      and RealAudio on
      the Internet

13.) True or False: Jesus' disciples wondered who would be the most important among themselves in heaven.

14.) Who did Jesus say would be the most
important disciple in heaven?

15.) When a person who was not a disciple cast out demons in Jesus' name,
the disciples
   a. told him to stop
   b. rejoiced
   c. told him to be wary of demons
   d. tried to take credit

16.) What did Jesus tell the disciples about the man casting out demons?

17.) Did you know it was God's plan for Jesus' death on the cross to take place in Jerusalem? Moses and Elijah talked to him about it during the transfiguration (Luke 9:30-31). Jesus set out for Jerusalem with God's plan in mind (Luke 9:51).

18.) True or False: When a village in Samaria refused to receive Jesus, the disciples pleaded with Jesus to forgive the people of the village.

19.) Concerning this village, Jesus told the disciples
   a. to set it on fire
   b. to rename it "Petra" after Peter
   c. not to be unforgiving toward the citizens of the town
   d. He would eat the Last Supper in this town

20.) True or False: After Jesus spoke to the people in the village, they decided to let Him pass through.

21.) Did you know that Jesus chose another seventy men to go before Him into each town He would be visiting? (Luke 10:1). Some Bibles give the number as seventy-two (Today's English Version).

22.) When visiting the towns, Jesus told the seventy workers to take
a. plenty of money
b. their credit cards
c. an angel on each shoulder
d. nothing

23.) How would the workers be taken care of?

24.) Jesus told the workers He was sending them out as
a. lambs among wolves
b. doves among hawks
c. sheep among lions
d. fish among sharks

25.) True or False: When the seventy returned to Jesus, they told Him they were amazed by the power Jesus had given them.

1.) Who told the story of the prodigal son?

2.) Where can you find the story of the prodigal son?

3.) True or False: Like many of Jesus' stories, the parable of the prodigal son appears more than once in the Bible.

4.) What does the word *prodigal* mean?

5.) In the story, how many sons did the wealthy man have?

6.) The younger son asked his father to
   a. give him his share of his inheritance
   b. let him marry the richest girl in town
   c. allow him to go to the skating rink with the church youth group
   d. loan him some money to go to the mall

7.) An *inheritance* is
  a. a hair transplant
  b. property that is passed on when someone dies
  c. nose hair
  d. Hebrew for "cash"

8.) True or False: The father did as the younger son asked.

9.) The younger son
  a. invested the money in comic books
  b. bought Mark McGwire's seventieth homerun baseball
  c. wasted his money
  d. buried the money in the backyard

10.) After the son's money was gone, he got a job
  a. at a fast-food restaurant
  b. herding sheep
  c. as a used-car salesman
  d. tending pigs

11.) Did you know that the younger son was about to starve from hunger before he finally decided to go back to his father and ask forgiveness? (Luke 15:17). The son's desperate state is much like the sad situation many sinners will come to before they repent and ask God for forgiveness.

12.) True or False: When the father saw the son returning, he was angry and told him to go back to tending pigs.

13.) When the son returned, the father gave him
a. a whipping
b. a video game
c. a job
d. a ring, a robe, and shoes

14.) True or False: The father threw a big party to celebrate.

15.) True or False: The father was so happy to have the younger brother home, he forgot all about the older brother.

16.) When the older son heard about the welcome-home party, he
   a. hired a band to play at the party
   b. hugged and kissed his brother
   c. gave his brother the keys to his car
   d. was angry

17.) Why did the older brother feel this way?

18.) The father said to the older brother,
   a. "Leave my house"
   b. "I always liked your younger brother better than you"
   c. "Everything I have is yours and we are close"
   d. "You always were a tattletale"

19.) True or False: The father convinced the older brother to celebrate his brother's homecoming.

THE GOOD SAMARITAN

1.) Where can you find the story of the
Good Samaritan?

2.) True or False: The parable of the
Good Samaritan can be found in all
four Gospels.

3.) Did you know that the Gospel of
John does not record any of Jesus'
parables?

4.) A parable is
a. a biography
b. a pair of pears
c. a story that teaches a lesson
d. a fable told by Aesop

5.) Jesus told the story of the Good
Samaritan to answer the question,
a. "Can I follow you?"
b. "What can I eat?"
c. "Is it okay for me to watch PG-13
movies?"
d. "Who is my neighbor?"

6.) Jesus was asked this question by
   a. a lawyer
   b. an evil woman
   c. Satan
   d. one of the Seven Dwarves

7.) In the story, a man needed help because he

   a. had eaten too much and needed to be carried
   b. didn't know who his neighbor was
   c. had been beaten and robbed
   d. refused to ask for directions even though he had been driving for hours

8.) True or False: When the priest and Levite saw the man lying on the side of the road, they stopped and helped him.

9.) To what city was the man going when he was beaten and robbed? Hint: The Jews had taken it by knocking down its walls with the sound of trumpets and a shout.

10.) Who stopped to help the injured man?

11.) Did you know that the road to Jericho was very dangerous? Thieves and bandits could hide in its mountainous terrain, waiting to rob travelers. This is probably why it is the setting for the parable of the Good Samaritan.

12.) Did you know that the Samaritan was an unlikely person to help a Jew? Jews were their hated enemies. This is demonstrated by the Samaritan village that refused to offer Jesus a place to stay when they discovered He was on His way to Jerusalem. Read Luke 9:51–56 to learn more.

13.) The salves the Samaritan applied to the man's wounds were
a. Solarcaine spray and Bactine
b. Dr. Feelgood's Miracle Salve and Potion
c. oil and wine
d. rubbing alcohol and butter

14.) True or False: The Samaritan stayed with the man the following day.

15.) The Samaritan took the man to
   a. dinner at Burger King
   b. a dark alley and robbed him
   c. an inn
   d. a revival meeting at church

16.) How much did the Samaritan give the innkeeper to care for the man until he was well?

17.) Did you know that two denarii was equal to two days' pay?

18.) True or False: Jesus asked the lawyer to identify which person was the man's neighbor.

19.) Who do you think was the neighbor to the man: the Levite, the priest, or the Samaritan?

20.) Jesus told the lawyer,
   a. "You are like the Levite"
   b. "Only good people are your neighbors"
   c. "You need to be concerned only about people who go to your school"
   d. "Go and do likewise"

1.) True or False: You can read about Jesus' resurrection in all four Gospels.

2.) Who were the three women who went to Jesus' grave the day He arose?

3.) When the women saw the grave, they discovered that the covering of the grave had been rolled back by
a. an angel of the Lord   c. Jesus
b. Goliath   d. Samson

4.) The one who rolled the stone back told the women,
a. "You will be punished for stealing the body"
b. "Expect an earthquake"
c. "Fear not, for Jesus has risen"
d. "I'm tired from all that work and I want something to eat"

5.) True or False: Jesus' disciples believed the women when they told them that Jesus had risen from the dead.

6.) Who went to the grave to see if what the women said was true?

7.) True or False: Jesus appeared to Mary Magdalene after He arose.

8.) When Jesus saw His disciples after He had risen, He said,
   a. "See, I told you so!"
   b. "Is there any bread left over from the Last Supper?"
   c. "Peace be unto you"
   d. "I really missed you these past three days"

9.) He said this because He
   a. wanted to show He was right
   b. was hungry
   c. wanted to reassure them
   d. was glad to be back

THE LORD'S PRAYER

1.) Did you know you can find The Lord's Prayer in two places in the Bible? You can read it in Matthew 6:9–13 and Luke 11:2–3.

2.) Can you recite The Lord's Prayer by heart?

3.) Jesus taught the disciples this prayer because

a. one of them had asked Him to teach them how to pray
b. He was angered by their awkward prayers
c. otherwise, they would sing psalms off-key
d. they needed a new version for Dial-a-Prayer

4.) According to The Lord's Prayer, where is God the Father?

5.) What does Jesus mean when He says God's name should be hallowed?

6.) What do you do to honor God's name?

7.) True or False: Obeying God's commandment not to take His name in vain is one way to keep God's name hallowed.

8.) True or False: In Matthew's Gospel, Jesus told them how to pray because He was angered by the hypocrites' loud praying.

9.) What is a hypocrite?

10.) Did you know that there is no contradiction between the two accounts of Jesus' sharing the prayer? The Lord's Prayer was apparently taught at two different times.

11.) True or False: Once you learn the Lord's Prayer, there is no need to pray on your own.

12.) The Lord's Prayer says to ask God for enough food every day. Can you remember the last time you were really hungry? Does remembering this make you think about how important it is to ask God to take care of you?

13.) Why is this prayer called the Lord's Prayer?

14.) When Jesus says we should ask God to forgive us as we forgive others, it means
   a. God should forgive us whether we forgive others or not
   b. we should not owe anyone any money
   c. we should not loan anyone any money
   d. God will forgive us when we forgive others

15.) True or False: You are supposed to pray the Lord's Prayer every day on the radio to show how wonderful you are.

PAUL SPEAKS ABOUT LOVE

1.) Who wrote 1 Corinthians?

2.) The Corinthians who received the letter were
   a. members of the Corinthian Country Club
   b. members of the church at Corinth
   c. makers of Corinthian leather
   d. reporters for the Corinthian Courant

3.) Did you know that in some older versions of the Bible, the word "charity" is used in place of the word "love" in Paul's first letter to the Corinthians? If you have ever heard someone speak of showing another person Christian charity, it means showing kindness and compassion.

4.) True or False: Fine preaching makes up for a lack of love.

5.) You don't need love if you have
  a. lots of money
  b. faith
  c. plenty of lambs to sacrifice
  d. none of the above. You must have love

6.) When Paul says love is not puffed up, he means love is not
  a. fat
  b. filled with air
  c. inflated like a blowfish
  d. proud

7.) What does Paul mean when he says that love is not provoked? (1 Corinthians 13:5)

8.) True or False: We know everything there is to know while we live on earth.

9.) Of faith, hope, and love, which is the greatest?

10.) Why do you think love is so important?

1.) The fruit of the Spirit is
   a. an orange
   b. a lemon
   c. a set of attitudes you'll have if you love God
   d. the title of a Dr. Seuss book

2.) Where in the Bible can we can learn about the fruit of the Spirit?

3.) Who told us about the fruit of the Spirit?

4.) The Galatians were
   a. members of a group of churches in Galatia
   b. a galaxy of stars
   c. bugs from a popular video game
   d. aliens from another galaxy

5.) Did you know that you cannot find Galatia on a modern-day map? Galatia was the name of a region in Asia Minor—modern-day Turkey.

6.) One fruit of the Spirit is "love." Can you name at least one other letter where Paul writes about love?

7.) When Paul speaks of joy, he means
a. a dishwashing detergent.
b. happiness in the Lord.
c. a baby kangaroo.
d. Joseph's nickname.

8.) Did you know there is more than one type of peace? You can be at peace with yourself, which means you like yourself. You can be at peace with others, which means you aren't fighting with anyone. On a national level, this means the country is not at war with another country. Most importantly, you can be at peace with the Lord. This does not mean you are perfect. When you are saved, you know the Lord has forgiven your sins. This puts you at peace with Him.

9.) You are long-suffering when
    a. you can sit through math class without passing a note.
    b. you don't fall asleep when the teacher is talking about history.
    c. you can forgive other people when they sin against you.
    d. you will eat vegetables three meals in a row.

10.) Paul names "gentleness" as a fruit of the Spirit (Galatians 5:22). Who is the most gentle person you know? What is he or she like?

11.) True or False: "Goodness" is a fruit of the Spirit.

12.) True or False: A person of faith must see something to believe it.

13.) *Meekness* means a person is
    a. a wimp.
    b. quiet.
    c. strong, but kind to others.
    d. mousy.

14.) The King James Version says that "temperance" is a fruit of the Spirit. Temperance is

a. another word for heating and cooling your house
b. running a fever
c. not going outside when it is too hot or too cold
d. controlling yourself and not going to the extreme

15.) True or False: Paul wrote about the fruit of the Spirit because he wanted everybody to live by the letter of the Mosaic law.

16.) Paul says that those living with the fruit of the Spirit have crucified the flesh. This means they

a. have Christian tattoos
b. have pierced their ears
c. have skin as wrinkled as a prune
d. don't think about their bodies as much as they think about living for Christ

17.) When we walk in the Spirit, it means that
   a. we obey Christ
   b. a cloud surrounds us
   c. we play basketball in high-heeled Easy Spirit pumps
   d. Mom won't drive us to soccer practice

18.) True or False: It is all right to be jealous of other people.

19.) Why is it important to obey Christ?

20.) Now that you have learned about the fruit of the Spirit, can you name all nine?

I PETER

1.) 1 Peter is a letter written by
   a. Peter   c. Mary
   b. Paul   d. Moses

2.) True or False: The author of 1 Peter was one of Jesus' apostles.

3.) Some scholars think that Peter was the leader of the apostles because he
   a. liked to write letters
   b. is named first in every list of the apostles in the Bible
   c. had the most money
   d. was the only one with Internet access

4.) Peter wrote this letter to
   a. Jesus
   b. persecuted Christians
   c. rich Christians
   d. a woman who wanted to publish his life story

5.) In 1 Peter 1:4, Peter speaks of an inheritance, meaning that the people he writes to will have
   a. their fortunes told
   b. more money in the future
   c. personal hair-dressers
   d. eternal life

6.) True or False:
Peter says that when we live like Jesus, we will not live like the rest of the world lives.

7.) What does the word *redeemed* mean?

8.) Peter says we were redeemed by
   a. Jesus
   b. silver
   c. a cents-off coupon
   d. the good things we do for others

9.) Peter says that Christians should not envy other people (1 Peter 2:1). Which of God's Ten Commandments means the same thing?

10.) We should also put aside evil speaking. What commandment does this remind you of?

11.) Peter says that Christians should be like
a. newborn babes
b. goats
c. sheep without a shepherd
d. Superman

12.) The milk of the word will
a. taste sour
b. turn to yogurt
c. spill on your books
d. make Christians grow

13.) Peter says that Christians are like
a. pet rocks
b. red bricks
c. living stones
d. wood

14.) True or False: Christians are building a spiritual house.

15.) Did you know that the name Peter means "rock"?

248

16.) True or False: Jesus is the chief cornerstone.

17.) What does Peter mean when he says that Jesus is the stone of stumbling and rock of offense?

18.) True or False: It is important for Christians to live as Christ wants because the world is watching us.

19.) Peter calls Christians "sojourners." What is a sojourner?

20.) True or False: When Peter compares Christians to pilgrims, he is talking about the people who sailed to America on the *Mayflower*.

21.) Christians should
   a. disobey all laws made by men
   b. obey the laws of their nations
   c. fight against the law
   d. obey the laws they think are right

22.) True or False: It is all right to be mean to someone who is mean to you first.

23.) When people say mean things to us, we should
   a. remember how Jesus trusted God
   b. gossip about them
   c. take them to court and let the judge decide what to do
   d. tell the teacher

24.) Peter compares the Christians to
   a. blocks of granite
   b. diamonds
   c. lost sheep
   d. all of the above

25.) Jesus spoke about lost sinners in three parables. Do you remember what they are?

26.) Peter refers to Jesus as a shepherd. What famous psalm also says He is a shepherd?

27.) What does the word *submit* mean?

28.) True or False: Peter says that wives should only submit to their husbands if the husbands follow Christ.

29.) Did you know that Peter offers hope to the wives of unsaved men? He tells them to obey God and to show their husbands how to live like Christians. Their lives may inspire their husbands to turn to Christ.

30.) True or False: Christian women should depend completely on lipstick, perfume,

and jewels to make them pretty.

31.) Peter tells husbands to
   a. give their wives anything they want
   b. take their wives out to dinner three times a week
   c. give their wives a dozen roses for every wedding anniversary
   d. honor their wives

32.) When Peter says that the wife is the weaker vessel, he means that the wife is
   a. not as strong physically as her husband
   b. dumb
   c. like a tiny blood vessel
   d. like a rowboat

33.) True or False: A Christian husband and wife are equal in that both will be given God's gift of salvation.

34.) True or False: Those who suffer because they are Christians are blessed.

35.) Peter says that Christians should answer questions about the Christian faith with
   a. anger   c. a funny greeting card
   b. meekness   d. an e-mail message

36.) Jesus spoke about suffering and meekness in a famous sermon. Do you remember the name of the sermon?

37.) Did you know that when Peter says, "Love will cover a multitude of sins," this is a quote from Proverbs 10:12?

38.) When Peter says that love will cover a multitude of sins, he means that
a. sleeping sins will stay warm.
b. a sinner can take refuge in a bomb shelter.
c. love has its limits.
d. when you love people, you can forget about their sins.

39.) True or False: Peter says that Christians should rejoice at being tried, because they share in suffering with Christ.

40.) In 1 Peter 4:15, Peter cautions Christians not to
a. be busybodies
b. be busy building up their bodies
c. busy themselves listening to hard-rock music
d. watch PG-rated movies

41.) Who are our earthly shepherds in the church today?

42.) Young people should submit to their
    a. impulse to play computer games all day
    b. elders
    c. sisters
    d. friends at school

43.) The Ten Commandments say, "Honor thy father and thy mother" (Exodus 20:12). How is this commandment like Peter's advice to young people?

44.) Who is the enemy of Christians?

45.) What is the last word in Peter's first letter?

1.) How do we know that Peter is the author of 2 Peter?

2.) Did you know that 2 Peter was written in AD 66, one year after 1 Peter was written?

3.) Peter wrote his second letter to
   a. Christians in Asia Minor
   b. Christians in the United States
   c. Jews in Israel
   d. Mrs. Witherspoon's fifth-grade class

4.) Why is it important for us to study Peter's letters?

5.) True or False: Peter says we are more like Jesus when we give up worldly things.

6.) Peter lists eight traits that a Christian should have. One of these is faith. Can you name the others?

7.) Did you know that Peter was probably over seventy years old and in a
Roman prison
when he wrote
this letter?

8.) When Peter
says "shortly
I must put off
this my taber-
nacle," he means that he
will soon
a. stop going to church
b. take his name out of the running
for church deacon
c. die
d. join another church

9.) True or False: Peter was an eyewit-
ness to God's confirmation that Jesus
is the Messiah.

10.) True or False: God will spare false
prophets.

11.) **False prophets**
   a. lie
   b. disrespect God
   c. tell people what they want to hear
   d. all of the above

12.) **An Old Testament false prophet, Balaam, the son of Beor, was rebuked by**
   a. a talking donkey
   b. the Apostle Peter
   c. a talking pig
   d. Joseph of Arimathea

13.) What does Peter mean when he says "a pig that has been washed goes back to roll in the mud"? (2 Peter 2:22, Today's English Version)

14.) **The Day of the Lord will arrive**
   a. as fast as a Domino's Pizza delivery guy
   b. as a thief in the night
   c. as soon as the circus comes to town
   d. absolutely, positively, on July 7, 2077

15.) True or False: Peter warns Christians not to fall away from the faith.

ANSWERS

THE CREATION AND THE FALL

1. Moses

2. He separated day and night (Genesis 1:3–5).

3. the sun, the moon, and the stars (Genesis 1:14-19)

5. to water the Garden (Genesis 2:10)

6. d) Adam (Genesis 2:19)

7. Adam (Genesis 2:19)

8. as a helpmate for Adam (Genesis 2:18)

9. c) Eve (Genesis 3:20)

11. a rib (Genesis 2:21)

13. a) serpent (Genesis 3:1)

14. d) knowledge of good and evil (Genesis 3:5)

16. They sewed themselves aprons made of fig leaves (Genesis 3:7).

17. They hid themselves (Genesis 3:8).

18. d) Eve (Genesis 3:12)

19. a) sent them out of Eden (Genesis 3:22–24)

20. cherubim (Genesis 3:24)

FIRST MURDER/THE FLOOD

1. Cain (Genesis 4:1)

2. Abel (Genesis 4:2)

4. b) Nod (Genesis 4:16)

6. Seth (Genesis 4:25)

7. Enoch (Genesis 5:22)

8. He walked with God (Genesis 5:22, 24).

9. d) 969 (Genesis 5:27)

10. c) an ark (Genesis 6:14)

12. 600 years old (Genesis 7:6)

13. a) Ham (Genesis 10:1)

15. the Pentateuch

A NEW WORLD

1. c) the Tower of Babel (Genesis 11:4)

2. He caused them to speak different languages and scattered them over the earth (Genesis 11:7–8).

4. the plain of Jordan (Genesis 13:10)

6. a) the mother of Ishmael (Genesis 16:15)

7. c) 86 (Genesis 16:16)

8. b) Abraham (Genesis 17:5)

9. Because He had promised to make him the father of many nations.

12. Moses

13. d) laughed (Genesis 17:17)

14. because Sarai was very old (Genesis 17:17)

15. a) Sodom and Gomorrah (Genesis 19:28)

16. She turned into a pillar of salt. (Genesis 19:26)

17. d) Her name is not recorded in the Bible.

19. a) Canaanites (Genesis 24:3)

20. d) gold jewelry (Genesis 24:22)

21. 14 years (Genesis 31:41)

22. Israel (Genesis 37:3)

23. a) was the child of his old age
(Genesis 37:3)

24. a coat of many colors (Genesis 37:3)

25. b) his brothers would serve Joseph
(Genesis 37:6–8)

26. stored food for the future (Genesis 41:48)

27. a) Joseph's death (Genesis 50:26)

ONE BIG EXIT

1. Moses

3. b) slaves (Exodus 1:11)

4. d) treasure cities (Exodus 1:11)

5. Pharoah's daughter (Exodus 2:5–6)

6. at the river, getting ready to take a bath
   (Exodus 2:5)

8. c) burning bush (Exodus 3:2)

9. b) a land flowing with milk and honey
   (Exodus 3:8)

10. a serpent (Exodus 4:3)

11. a) blood (Exodus 7:20)

13. d) silver and gold (Exodus 11:2)

14. Passover (Exodus 12:27)

15. the parting of the Red Sea
    (Exodus 14:13–31)

16. d) Moses

17. No. They were to gather twice their daily
    allotment on the day before the Sabbath.
    (Exodus 16:5)

18. because the Israelites complained
    (Exodus 16:12)

19. c) quail (Exodus 16:13)

20. b) the Ten Commandments (Exodus 20)

21. a) Aaron (Exodus 28:1)

22. b) a golden calf (Exodus 32:4)

23. d) Pentateuch

24. manna (Exodus 16:31)

25. cherubs and cherubim (Exodus 37:8–9)

1. In the book of Judges.

2. Judges ruled Israel.

4. d) wine or strong drink (Judges 13:4 and 7)

5. a) Samson's father Manoah (Judges 13:11–16)

6. It was a secret (Judges 13:18).

7. d) Philistine (Judges 14:3)

8. a) killed it with his bare hands (Judges 14:5–6)

9. c) a swarm of bees and honey (Judges 14:8)

10. He challenged them to solve a riddle (Judges 14:13).

11. b) Samson's wife (Judges 14:17)

12. a) Samson's friend (Judges 14:20)

14. d) donkey's jawbone (Judges 15:16)

15. He went to the next Philistine town, slew
    30 men, and took their cloaks (Judges
    14:19).

16. d) the donkey's jawbone (Judges 15:19)

17. a) 1100 pieces of silver each (Judges 16:5)

20. (c) tied with seven green cords of rope
    Judges 16:7)

21. c) new rope that had never been used
    (Judges 16:11)

22. He told her that his hair had to be woven
    in seven strands into the web of a loom
    (Judges 16:13).

23. He broke free easily (Judges 16).

24. b) pestered Samson every day to tell her
    until he confessed (Judges 16:16)

25. It began to grow again (Judges 16:22) .

27. b) was no longer walking with the Lord

28. Because Samson had been captured
(Judges 16:23–24)

29. 3000 (Judges 16:27)

30. b) prayed to God for strength (Judges
16:28–30)

31. He killed everyone at the gathering. In
death, Samson killed more Philistines
than he had at any time in his life.
(Judges 16:30)

RUTH

1. No

3. d) There wasn't enough food to eat because of famine (Ruth 1:1).

4. a) Moab (Ruth 1:2)

5. Bethlehem-judah (Ruth 1:1)

6. Ruth (Ruth 1:14)

7. b) Orpah and Ruth (Ruth 1:4)

8. ten years (Ruth 1:4–5)

9. d) return to her homeland (Ruth 1:7)

10. a) go back and live with their mothers (Ruth 1:8)

11. He died (Ruth 1:3).

13. d) convert to Judaism (Ruth 1:16)

14. a) changed her name to Mara (Ruth 1:20)

15. barley (Ruth 1:22)

16. gleaned the fields (Ruth 2:2)

18. a) Naomi's husband (Ruth 2:3)

19. a) that she would be safe and have plenty of water to drink (Ruth 2:9)

20. d) had taken good care of Naomi (Ruth 2:10–11)

21. (barley and wheat Ruth 2:23)

22. No.

23. a) ask Boaz what to do next (Ruth 3:1–4)

24. a) six measures of barley (Ruth 3:17)

25. the property that had belonged to Naomi's sons and husband (Ruth 4:9)

26. b) Ruth was a Moabite (Ruth 4:5–6)

27. a) accept Ruth as one of their own (Ruth 4:11)

28. c) married Ruth (Ruth 4:13)

30. sixty-six

2. a) she had no children (I Samuel 1:8)

3. She asked to give birth to a son (I Samuel 1:11).

4. b) that her son would belong to God (I Samuel 1:11)

5. d) cut (I Samuel 1:11)

6. Hannah gave birth to a son (I Samuel 1:20).

8. a) Eli the priest (I Samuel 1:25)

10. She wanted him to serve the Lord all of his life (I Samuel 1:28).

11. c) evil (I Samuel 2:12)

12. a) ministered before the Lord (I Samuel 2:18)

13. c) little coat (I Samuel 2:19)

14. a) blessed Hannah and her husband, Elkanah (I Samuel 2:20)

15. (I Samuel 3:8–10) Samuel answered the Lord on the fourth call.

16. yes (I Samuel 2:21)

18. The Lord said that both of them would die (I Samuel 2:34).

19. a) evil (I Samuel 3:3)

20. d) raise up His own priest who would do His will (I Samuel 2:35)

21. a) Eli (I Samuel 3:5)

22. a) sleeping (I Samuel 3:2)

23. d) punish Eli's house because Eli's sons were evil (I Samuel 3:11–14)

24. b) prophet (I Samuel 3:20)

FROM JUDGES TO A KING

2. b) made his sons judges in his place
   (I Samuel 8:1)

3. a) took bribes and did not rule fairly
   (I Samuel 8:3)

4. Joel and Abiah (I Samuel 8:2).

5. yes (I Samuel 8:3)

7. b) prayed to the Lord (I Samuel 8:6)

8. a) let the people see how a king would
   rule (I Samuel 8:9)

9. the Lord Himself (I Samuel 8:7)

10. a) greedy (I Samuel 8:10–17)

11. No. They still wanted a king
    (I Samuel 8:19).

12. Saul

14. d) being the tallest and most handsome
    man in all of Israel (I Samuel 9:2)

15. a) his father's lost donkeys (I Samuel 9:3)

17. (b) God had told Samuel in his ear that
    Saul was the one I Samuel 9:15–17).

18. d) was from the smallest of the twelve
    tribes of Israel, and his family was not
    important (I Samuel 9:21)

19. Samuel told Saul that the donkeys had
    been found (I Samuel 9:20).

20. Samuel anointed Saul king (I Samuel 10:1).

21. young women drawing water from the
    well (I Samuel 9:11)

23. b) prophecy (I Samuel 10:10)

24. No. The anointing had taken place
    privately (I Samuel 10:16).

YOUNG BLOOD

1. Because Saul disobeyed God (I Samuel 15:23)

3. a) handsome (I Samuel 16:6)

4. d) hearts (I Samuel 16:7)

5. Jesse (I Samuel 16:1)

6. seven (I Samuel 16:10)

7. b) glowing with health and handsome to look at (I Samuel 16:12)

8. The Lord told Samuel to anoint David king (I Samuel 16:12).

9. Because God had sent an evil spirit to bother rebellious Saul (I Samuel 16:15–17).

10. d) harp (I Samuel 16:16)

11. David (I Samuel 16:12)

13. (a) loved Saul and became his armor-bearer I Samuel 16:21)

14. a Philistine giant from Gath who taunted the Israelites (I Samuel 17:4)

16. the three eldest brothers, Eliab, Abinadab, and Shammah (I Samuel 17:13)

17. d) fed his father's sheep in Bethlehem (I Samuel 17:15)

18. forty (I Samuel 17:16)

19. a) take them food (I Samuel 17:17–18)

20. d) Goliath's challenge to the army (I Samuel 17:23)

21. c) riches, Saul's daughter, and freedom (I Samuel 17:25)

22. c) fight Goliath (I Samuel 17:32)

23. c) killed a lion and a bear who tried to steal his father's sheep (I Samuel 17:34–36)

24. David had faith that the Lord would keep him safe (I Samuel 17:37).

25. five (I Samuel 17:40)

26. b) made fun of David (I Samuel 17:42–43)

27. c) everyone would know about God
    (I Samuel 17:46)

29. They ran away (I Samuel 17:51).

30. He was angry. Eliab accused David of
    being naughty and only wanting to
    see the excitement. Eliab also feared
    that David had left the family's sheep
    untended (I Samuel 17:28).

THE KINGS RULE

2. He is old and ill (I Kings 1:1).

3. c) Solomon's older half-brother
   (I Kings 1:5)

4. a) he would be the next king (I Kings 1:5)

6. no (I Kings 1:6)

7. a) handsome (I Kings 1:6)

8. Bathsheba (I Kings 1:11)

9. a) speak to King David about Adonijah
   (I Kings 1:13)

10. d) Solomon was supposed to be the next
    king, not Adonijah (I Kings 1:13)

11. no (I Kings 1:18)

12. Solomon (I Kings 1:10)

14. a) had Solomon anointed and declared
    king (I Kings 1:33–34)

15. King David's own mule (I Kings 1:38).

16. a) trumpet (I Kings 1:39)

17. Jonathan (I Kings 1:43)

18. b) King David (I Kings 1:47)

19. He had seen the events with his own eyes
    (I Kings 1:48).

20. d) rose up and left the party in fear
    (I Kings 1:49)

21. a) begged King Solomon not to kill him
    (I Kings 1:51)

22. d) proved himself worthy (I Kings 1:52)

23. Adonijah would die (I Kings 1:52).

24. d) "Go to thine house" (I Kings 1:53).

2. c) disobeyed him (Esther 1:12)

3. b) women were to honor men and
   men were to rule their households
   (Esther 1:20–22)

4. because of her great beauty (Esther 1:11)

5. so he could find a new queen (Esther 2:4)

7. a) cousin (Esther 2:7)

8. b) she was an orphan (Esther 2:7)

9. d) We don't know

10. crowned her the new queen (Esther 2:17)

11. that she was Jewish (Esther 2:10)

12. because Mordecai told her not to
    (Esther 2:10)

13. b) telling him through Esther that his
    life was in danger from assassins
    (Esther 2:21–22)

14. a) was Jewish (Esther 3:4)

15. destroy them (Esther 3:9)

17. d) fine raiment (Esther 4:4)

18. The king had not summoned her, so asking to speak to him was risking her life (Esther 4:11).

19. a) fast for three days and nights (Esther 4:16)

20. d) Haman (Esther 5:12)

21. a) couldn't sleep (Esther 6:1)

22. honor Mordecai (Esther 6:3)

23. a) ring (Esther 8:2)

24. Haman (Esther 6:6)

25. Haman (Esther 7:6)

26. b) held a golden scepter toward her (Esther 8:4)

27. the Feast of Purim (Esther 9:19, 26)

29. the fourteenth and fifteenth days of Adar (Esther 9:21)

2. a) Uz (Job 1:1)

3. ten; seven sons and three daughters
    (Job 1:2)

4. d) curse God (Job 1:11)

5. d) spare Job's life (Job 2:6)

6. c) sores (Job 2:7)

7. b) curse God and die (Job 2:9)

8. three friends (Job 2:11)

9. to make a burnt offering of seven bulls
    and seven rams (Job 42:8)

10. a) comfort Job (Job 2:11)

11. d) angry about their unfaithfulness to Him
    (Job 42:7)

12. 140 (Job 42:16)

13. a) gave him twice as much as he had
    before his suffering (Job 42:10)

14. a) three daughters and seven sons
   (Job 42:12)

15. d) beauty (Job 42:15)

BITS OF WISDOM

1. a) a king of Israel (Proverbs 1:1)

2. the Lord (Proverbs 2:6)

3. d) evil (Proverbs 3:7)

4. a) shows you right from wrong
   (Proverbs 3:12)

5. wisdom (Proverbs 3:13)

6. a) work (Proverbs 6:6–8)

7. b) seven (Proverbs 6:16)

8. b) bad women (Proverbs 6:24)

10. d) sister (Proverbs 7:4)

12. c) rubies (Proverbs 8:11)

13. Solomon wrote most of it, although some
    portions are attributed to others.

15. wisdom

16. b) love you (Proverbs 9:8)

17. Because the wise person is always trying to be wiser. Learning from others is a way to do that.

18. yes (Proverbs 9:11)

19. c) love (Proverbs 10:12)

20. yes (Proverbs 11:13)

21. Speaking badly of others is hurtful, and gossip is not always true. Have you ever been hurt by something someone said about you?

22. a) poverty and shame (Proverbs 13:18)

23. c) honor (Proverbs 13:18)

24. Give the person a kind answer (Proverbs 15:1).

25. d) honeycomb (Proverbs 16:24)

26. his grandchildren (Proverbs 17:6)

27. a) tell lies (Proverbs 19:5)

29. It means that God does not want people to cheat each other. For instance, God would not want a butcher to charge you for two pounds of meat when he is only selling you one.

30. because a foolish person does not appreciate good advice (Proverbs 23:9)

31. a) will have no reward (Proverbs 24:19–20)

32. d) only buy as many things as you need and no more (Proverbs 25:16)

33. He would say that riches are not forever (Proverbs 27:24).

34. c) give him bread to eat (Proverbs 25:21)

35. no (Proverbs 26:19)

36. King Solomon was very wealthy. Solomon spoke of his riches in Ecclesiastes. Even Jesus referred to Solomon's riches (Matthew 6:29).

37. d) give to the poor (Proverbs 28:27)

38. c) stirs up even more anger (Proverbs 29:22)

39. Thirty-nine

THE GOOD WIFE

1. a) virtuous (Proverbs 31:10)

2. A favorable character trait such as honesty, charity, thrift, or integrity; Christian behavior.

3. rubies (Proverbs 31:10)

4. c) heart (Proverbs 31:11)

5. wool and flax (Proverbs 31:13)

6. her husband and children (Proverbs 31:28)

7. c) works willingly (Proverbs 31:13)

8. from far away (Proverbs 31:14)

9. a) before dawn (Proverbs 31:15)

10. willingness to work; the work ethic (Proverbs 31:14–19)

11. d) charity (Proverbs 31:20)

12. b) she has plenty of clothing to keep her family warm

13. purple (Proverbs 31:22)

15. fine linen (Proverbs 31:24)

16. d) strength and honor (Proverbs 31:25)

17. wisdom (Proverbs 31:26)

18. c) is not vain or conceited (Proverbs 31:30)

19. fear of the Lord (Proverbs 31:30)

20. She will be praised (Proverbs 31:30).

1. Daniel

3. d) to be excused from eating food
   forbidden under Jewish dietary laws
   (Daniel 1:8)

4. favor and compassion (Daniel 1:9)

5. understanding of visions and dreams
   (Daniel 1:17)

7. that they all should be killed (Daniel 2:12)

8. a) asked the king for more time and
   prayed to God for wisdom (Daniel
   2:16–18)

9. gold (Daniel 3:1)

11. c) thrown into a fiery furnace (Daniel 3:6)

12. a) went to live with the beasts of the field,
    eating grass for food (Daniel 4:32–33)

14. He praised other gods (Daniel 5:4).

15. a) with handwriting on a wall (Daniel 5:5)

16. Daniel (Daniel 5:12)

17. (the queen Daniel 5:10)

18. no (Daniel 3:18)

19. God delivered them (Daniel 3:25).

THE UNWILLING SERVANT

1. Jonah

3. Ninevah (Jonah 1:2)

4. c) Joppa (Jonah 1:3)

5. b) on a ship heading to Tarshish
(Jonah 1:3)

7. a great wind (Jonah 1:4)

8. a) their gods (Jonah 1:5)

9. d) throw him overboard (Jonah 1:12)

10. No. They tried to row to land first but
failed because of the rough waters
(Jonah 1:13).

12. d) grew calm (Jonah 1:15)

13. He prayed (Jonah 2:1).

14. b) go to Ninevah (Jonah 3:1–2)

16. three days and three nights (Jonah 1:17)

17. that Ninevah would be overthrown in forty
    days (Jonah 3:4)

18. a) fasted and wore sackcloth (Jonah 3:5)

19. c) ashes (Jonah 3:6)

20. He did not destroy them, but let them live
    (Jonah 3:10).

22. b) was angry (Jonah 4:1)

24. to see what would happen to the city
    (Jonah 4:5)

25. d) gourd (Jonah 4:6)

26. angry (Jonah 4:9)

27. that if he could feel pity for a plant, he
    should love the people living in Ninevah
    (Jonah 4:10–11)

29. c) sixty-six books

MATTHEW'S GOSPEL

1. Matthew

3. d) Jesus' birth line, or genealogy

5. Bethlehem (Matthew 2:l)

7. d) kill Jesus (Matthew 2:13)

8. a) Egypt (Matthew 2:13)

9. d) locusts and wild honey (Matthew 3:4)

11. forty days and forty nights (Matthew 4:2)

12. men (or people) (Matthew 4:19)

13. a) Beatitudes

15. the Lord's Prayer (Matthew 6:9–13)

16. d) heaven (Matthew 6:20)

18. the Golden Rule (Matthew 7:12)

19. d) mother-in-law (Matthew 8:14)

20. parables

21. twelve

22. a) ghost (Matthew 14:26)

23. a) great faith (Matthew 15:28)

24. yes (Matthew 20:17–19)

25. b) we don't know when the Lord will
    return (Matthew 24:42)

26. Judas Iscariot (Matthew 26:14–15)

27. d) thirty pieces of silver (Matthew 26:15)

28. the Garden of Gethsemane (Matthew
    26:36)

29. a) slept (Matthew 26:40, 43)

30. (Matthew 26:48) b) kissing Him

31. a) repented (Matthew 27:3)

33. "Truly this was the Son of God" (Matthew
    27:54).

34. d) an angel (Matthew 28:2)

35. a) Galilee (Matthew 28:10)

36. from the mouth of a fish (Matthew 17:27)

38. They were bribed by the chief priests and elders to say that Jesus' disciples stole His body (Matthew 28:11–15).

39. That He is the Son of God.

40. "Amen."

JOHN'S JOURNEY WITH JESUS

1. John

3. c) Cana (John 2:1)

4. His mother (John 2:3)

5. c) wedding (John 2:1)

7. d) overturned their tables and angrily rebuked them (John 2:15)

8. b) eternal life (John 3:16)

9. a drink of water (John 4:7)

10. that He is the Messiah (John 4:26)

11. a) five barley loaves and two small fish (John 6:9)

12. 5,000 (John 6:10)

13. a) Judas Iscariot (John 12:4)

14. He washed their feet (John 13:14).

15. to serve one another (John 13:14)

17. yes (John 13:38)

18. c) rooster crowed (John 18:27)

20. d) "Crucify Him!" (John 19:15)

21. We will keep His commandments (John 14:15).

22. Jesus of Nazareth, King of the Jews (John 19:19)

24. "It is finished" (John 19:30).

25. a) Why weepest thou? (John 20:13)

26. Woman, why weepest thou? (John 20:15)

27. No. He wanted proof (John 20:25).

28. d) the Son of God, who is worthy to be worshiped (John 30:31)

29. d) believe in Jesus Christ, the Son of God, and have life in His name (John 20:31)

30. "Amen."

NEWS FOR THE ROMANS

1. Paul the Apostle

2. a) Roman Christians (Romans 1:7)

4. d) Jesus Christ our Lord, the Son of God
   (Romans 1:3)

5. Jesus' resurrection from the dead
   (Romans 1:4)

7. d) faith in our Lord Jesus Christ
   (Romans 5:1)

8. d) nothing. His gift of salvation is free
   (Romans 5:18).

9. Jesus Christ, the Son of God (Romans
   5:21)

11. a) the New Covenant (Hebrews 8:13)

12. d) the Holy Spirit (Romans 8:1)

13. life and peace (Romans 8:6)

14. no (Romans 3:10)

15. The Holy Spirit tells God what the Christian needs (Romans 8:26).

16. b) God's (Romans 8:27)

17. d) nothing (Romans 8:35–39)

18. He means that the Gospel is for everyone, not just a certain group (Romans 9:24).

20. Benjamin (Romans 11:1)

21. a) God has not forgotten His chosen people (Romans 11:2)

22. c) Gentiles (Romans 11:13)

23. the Gentiles (Romans 11:13)

25. d) we should use whatever gifts God gave us (Romans 12:3–8)

26. God (Romans 12:19)

27. d) good (Romans 12:21)

28. Jesus Christ (Romans 14:10)

29. "Amen" (Romans 16:27).

THE THESSALONIANS

1. Paul the Apostle

2. b) Thessalonica

4. a) church (I Thessalonians 1:1)

6. a) praises them (I Thessalonians 1:3)

7. d) worry about pleasing God, not people
   (I Thessalonians 2:4)

8. Satan (I Thessalonians 2:18)

10. a) love one another (I Thessalonians 4:9)

11. c) the breastplate of faith and love
    and a helmet of hope and salvation
    (I Thessalonians 5:8)

12. He told us to comfort each other.

13. pray (I Thessalonians 5:17)

14. a) evil (I Thessalonians 5:22)

15. d) "Amen."

HEBREWS

1. We do not know, although some Bible scholars think Paul the Apostle wrote it.

3. a) letter

4. d) through His Son Jesus (Hebrews 1:1–2)

5. Jesus (Hebrews 2:13)

6. eternal salvation; everlasting life (Hebrews 5:8–9)

7. ministering spirits (Hebrews 1:14)

8. b) mercy and grace (Hebrews 4:16)

9. a) faith (Hebrews 6:1)

10. He will not forget them (Hebrews 6:10).

12. d) faith (Hebrews 11:6)

13. Abel, Enoch, Noah, Abraham, Sarah, Isaac, Jacob, Joseph, the parents of Moses, Moses, Rahab (Hebrews 11)

14. He sits at the right hand of the throne of God (Hebrews 12:2).

15. "Amen."

16. continual praise (Hebrews 13:15)

17. c) wants us to learn how to be holy (Hebrews 12:10)

18. d) holiness (Hebrews 12:14)

19. a) angels (Hebrews 13:2)

20. We should ignore strange teachings because any teaching about God that does not come from the Bible is false. Jesus Christ never changes. His Word stays the same (Hebrews 13:8–9).

JOHN'S LETTERS

1. A letter

2. three

3. d) John the Apostle

4. a) ourselves (I John 1:8)

6. that we should love one another
   (I John 3:11)

7. a) sent His only begotten Son into the
   world, that we might live through Him
   (I John 4:9)

8. d) the world (I John 2:15)

9. a) love (I John 2:5)

10. God is Love (I John 4:8).

11. God will live in them, and they will live in
    God (I John 4:15).

12. People who love God love their brother (I
    John 4:21).

14. d) idols (I John 5:21)

15. "Amen."

17. grace, mercy, and peace (2 John 1:3)

18. a) not let the person into your house
(2 John 1:7–10)

19. Because if you do, you will be just as bad
as the false Christian (2 John 1:11).

20. Because he hopes to see his readers in
person soon (2 John 1:12).

21. d) "Amen."

23. John wished Gaius prosperity and health
(3 John 1:2).

24. a) a strong Christian who walked in the
truth (3 John 1:3)

25. a) was more concerned about his reputation than he was about other Christians
(3 John 1:9)

26. people who do evil (3 John:11)

27. good (3 John 1:11)

28. c) was a true Christian witness
(3 John 1:12)

29. d) hoped to see them in person soon
(3 John 1:13–14)

30. peace (3 John 1:14)

A WORD FROM JUDE

1. Jude

3. a) Christians in the early church (Jude 1:1)

4. mercy, peace, and love (Jude 1:2)

5. b) denied our Lord God and His Son Jesus Christ (Jude 1:4)

6. (Jude 1:7) Sodom and Gomorrah

7. b) Cain (Jude 1:11)

8. d) will say nice things they don't mean to important people who can help them (Jude 1:16)

9. Proverbs

10. "Amen." (Jude 1:25)

11. a) are more interested in worldly things like being rich and popular than in God (Jude 1:18)

12. They can pray in the Holy Spirit (Jude 1:20).

13. d) in God's love (Jude 1:21)

14. eternal life (Jude 1:21)

15. God (Jude 1:25)

1. a. Genesis. The story is told in chapters 6–9.

2. False. God was angry that the people were so evil (Genesis 6:5–6).

3. b. destroy all the people, animals, and birds He had created (Genesis 6:7).

4. True (Genesis 6:9–10).

5. Noah had three sons (Genesis 6:9).

6. Noah's three sons were named Shem, Ham, and Japheth (Genesis 6:9).

8. A ritually clean beast is acceptable to God for sacrifice. A ritually unclean beast is not. Although God asked for animal sacrifices under Old Testament law, Christians do not make animal sacrifices. Instead, we give money to the work of the church. It is also important to give our time to the church. We can do that by helping with vacation Bible school, babysitting in the nursery, or in other ways. How can you help your Sunday school teacher or other adults in church?

9. c. 600 years old (Genesis 7:6).

10. It rained forty days and forty nights (Genesis 7:12).

12. a. 7 1/2 months. The Flood began on the seventeenth day of the second month (Genesis 7:11). And Noah was able to see the tops of the mountains again on the first day of the tenth month (Genesis 8:5).

14. False. The first bird Noah sent out from the ark was a raven (Genesis 8:7).

15. d. an olive branch (Genesis 8:11). This showed Noah that the water had started to go down.

16. True (Genesis 8:13).

17. c. built an altar to God and made sacrifices upon it (Genesis 8:20).

18. True (Genesis 8:21 and 9:11).

19. God was pleased with the smell of the sacrifices Noah made after the flood. The

pleasant odor caused Him to promise not
to destroy the earth by flood again
(Genesis 8:20–22).

20. A rainbow reminds us of God's promise
(Genesis 9:13).

A TOWERING PROBLEM

1. The story of the Tower of Babel can be found in Genesis 11:1–9.

2. True (Genesis 11:1).

3. d. an unspecified language. Everyone spoke the same language (Genesis 11:1), but the Bible does not say what language the people spoke.

5. c. brick (Genesis 11:3).

6. True (Genesis 11:4–5).

7. d. reach to heaven (Genesis 11:6).

8. False (Genesis 11:6–7).

9. d. made the people all speak different languages so they couldn't finish the work (Genesis 11:7).

10. The story of the Tower of Babel is important because:
    1. It shows us that God places limits upon mankind (Genesis 11:6).
    2. It explains why we speak different languages (Genesis 11:6–9).

3. It shows how God scattered the people all over the face of the earth (Genesis 11:9).

2. You can find the story of God's promise to Abraham in Genesis 16–19.

3. True (Genesis 17:4–5).

4. Abraham was ninety-nine years old when God appeared to him (Genesis 17:1).

5. c. obey Him (Genesis 17:1).

6. b. bowed down, touching his face to the ground (Genesis 17:3).

7. A covenant is a solemn promise. For example, when we are baptized, we promise God we will follow Him.

8. True (Genesis 17:2).

9. a. a member of a future generation.

10. d. the land of Canaan (Genesis 17:8). Abraham was living in Canaan as a foreigner at that time.

11. True. The covenant applied to Abraham and to future generations as well (Genesis 17:8).

12. c. Abraham was to be the father of many nations (Genesis 17:5).

13. True (Genesis 17:6).

14. True (Genesis 17:7).

15. Abraham's wife was named Sarai before God renamed her Sarah (Genesis 17:15).

16. c. have a baby (Genesis 17:16).

17. b. laughed (Genesis 17:17). Abraham did not think it was possible for him and his wife to be new parents because they were old.

18. God promised a baby boy (Genesis 17:16).

19. c. was ninety years old, which is usually too old to have a baby (Genesis 17:17).

20. Abraham was ninety-nine years old when God promised him a baby (Genesis 17:17).

22. c. a person who receives an inheritance. In biblical times, the firstborn son usually was next in line for his father's position and money when the father died. This meant that after the father died, the oldest son became head of the family.

23. False (Genesis 17:19).

24. True (Genesis 17:13).

25. Like Abraham, Christians are people of
    God. We are Abraham's descendants.

2. False: Exodus and Deuteronomy are both Old Testament books. Exodus is the second book of the Bible, and Deuteronomy is the fifth book.

3. Moses wrote the first five books of the Bible.

5. The five books of the Pentateuch are Genesis, Exodus, Leviticus, Numbers, and Deuteronomy.

6. b. Mount Sinai (Exodus 19:20).

8. b. been brought out of slavery in Egypt. You can read about this event in Exodus 5:1–15:21.

9. True (Exodus 20:3; Deuteronomy 5:7).

10. The First Commandment is the most important because it defines our relationship to God. God wants us to love Him, just as He loves us. If we do not love God, we can not keep the other commandments.

11. False. The Second Commandment tells us not to make any idols (Exodus 20:4; Deuteronomy 5:8–9).

12. God means we are not to call His name unless we are praying to Him or worshipping Him. Think about how you would feel if people kept saying your name, attracting your attention for no reason. Would you feel angry? Would you be upset? God does not want us to call His name unless we mean to speak to Him or to praise His name.

13. d. keep holy, cease work, and remember His people's deliverance from Egypt (Exodus 20:8–11; Deuteronomy 5:12–15).

14. False (Exodus 20:8–11; Deuteronomy 5:12–15). However, Jesus said that necessary work may be done on the Sabbath (Matthew 12:1–8; Mark 2:23–27; Luke 6:1–5).

15. God wants us to rest every seventh day because He rested on the seventh day after He created the world (Exodus 20:11). By resting on the seventh day, we are honoring God by being like Him in this way.

319

17. We attend church on Sunday, read the Bible, rest, and otherwise follow God's instructions.

18. c. father and mother (Exodus 20:12; Deuteronomy 5:16). Our parents have an important place in our lives because God has entrusted them to care for us on earth. God wants us to give them special respect and honor. However, we should also treat our teachers, pastor, and friends with respect.

19. True (Exodus 20:13; Deuteronomy 5:17). Life belongs to God the Creator, not to us.

20. We can find out how God established marriage in Genesis 2:21–34.

21. c. steal (Exodus 20:15; Deuteronomy 5:19). Showing love for others includes respecting the things they own. That is why we should not rob people.

22. We should not lie, but tell the truth. Giving false information is a sin against the person we're lying to. Lies hurt other people. A liar is not showing love to God or to other people.

24. d. wish we had our neighbor's stuff. Do you know someone who would like something you have, such as a movie video or a computer game? Why not share it with that person? You may make a new friend.

25. a. Leviticus.

27. b. stone tablets (Deuteronomy 5:22).

28. False. While Moses was with God on the mountain for forty days, the people made a false idol. Moses was so angry with their disobedience to God, he broke the tablets when he came down the mountain (Deuteronomy 9:17).

29. These are the Ten Commandments:
    1. Worship no god but God.
    2. Do not worship idols.
    3. Do not take the Lord's name in vain.
    4. Remember the Sabbath Day and keep it holy.
    5. Honor your mother and father.
    6. Do not murder.
    7. Do not commit adultery.
    8. Do not steal.
    9. Do not lie.
    10. Do not covet.

2. True (Numbers 27:18–23).

4. c. the death of Moses.

5. The book of Joshua is found in the Old Testament.

6. As its title suggests, Joshua wrote the book of Joshua.

7. c. Jordan River (Joshua 1:2).

8. True (Joshua 1:9).

9. c. the home of a wicked woman (Joshua 2:1).

10. True (Joshua 2:2–7).

12. a. on the roof (Joshua 2:6).

14. True (Joshua 2:10–14).

15. Rahab protected the spies because she knew they were there to claim the land for the Lord's people (Joshua 2:9).

17. The ark of the covenant was a wooden box covered with gold and built to God's specification. It contained the stone tablets on which the Ten Commandments were written.

18. A total of forty thousand men crossed the plains of Jericho, ready to fight for the Lord (Joshua 4:13).

19. b. eaten food grown in the Promised Land (Joshua 5:11).

20. Manna was the food God rained down upon the Israelites to provide food for them while they were wandering in the wilderness on their way to the Promised Land. God rained fresh manna for them every day (Exodus 16:14–18).

22. False. The walls came tumbling down by the sounds of horns and a shout. The priests blew horns for seven days as they walked around the city with the ark of the covenant (Joshua 6:3–16).

23. The lives of Rahab and her household were spared during the fall of Jericho.

This is important because it shows God always keeps His promises (Joshua 6:17 and 22–23).

24. b. put into the Lord's treasury (Joshua 6:19).

25. True (Joshua 6:27).

DAVID FIGHTS GOLIATH

1. a. 1 Samuel. Look in Chapter 17, verses 1–54.

3. False. Goliath wore bronze armor all over his body. A soldier went before him to carry his shield. Goliath carried a large spear (1 Samuel 17:5–7).

4. False. They were too scared to fight Goliath (1 Samuel 17:11).

5. David was taking food to his three older brothers who were soldiers in battle (1 Samuel 17:17).

6. b. tended sheep (1 Samuel 17:15).

7. Gath was located in Philistia.

8. True (1 Samuel 17:23).

10. False. Eliab, the oldest, scolded David and asked him who was tending his sheep (1 Samuel 17:28).

11. a. wondered how Goliath dared to defy the army of the living God (1 Samuel 17:26).

12. c. was only a boy (1 Samuel 17:33).

14. True (1 Samuel 17:36).

15. c. he couldn't walk in it because he wasn't used to such cumbersome armor (1 Samuel 17:39).

16. David picked up five stones (1 Samuel 17:40).

17. False. Goliath made fun of David (1 Samuel 17:43–44).

18. d. there is a God in Israel (1 Samuel 17:46).

19. True. The stone hit his forehead, and Goliath fell face down to the ground (1 Samuel 17:49).

20. a. chased the Philistines back to their own country (1 Samuel 17:52).

ELISHA PERFORMS MANY MIRACLES

1. False (1 Kings 19:19).

2. b. 2 Kings.

4. Enoch was taken to heaven without dying because he walked with the Lord (Genesis 5:23–24).

5. True (2 Kings 2:9).

6. b. dividing the Jordan River and walking on dry land (2 Kings 2:14). He struck the water with Elijah's cloak, and the water parted.

7. True (2 Kings 2:15). This is important because their recognition of him helped to establish Elisha as a prophet.

8. c. made the water pure (2 Kings 2:20–22).

9. c. bald (2 Kings 2:23).

11. c. rebelled against Israel (2 Kings 3:5).

12. True (2 Kings 3:16).

13. c. they thought the water they saw around the camp was blood (2 Kings 3:21-23). When the Moabites saw water on what had been dry land, they thought it was blood because the sunlight hit it in such a way that the water appeared to be red. They thought the three armies had killed each other, so they decided to rob the camp.

14. They were attacked by the Israelites (2 Kings 3:24).

15. True (2 Kings 3:24-25).

16. a. was in debt (2 Kings 4:1).

17. d. a small jar of olive oil (2 Kings 4:2). Elisha told her to get jars from her neighbors and pour the oil into them (2 Kings 4:3).

18. The woman poured the small amount of olive oil she had in her house into all the jars. When they were all filled, the oil stopped.

19. True (2 Kings 4:7). She sold the oil for money.

20. No, she did not accept his offer (2 Kings 4:13).

21. b. promising her that she would have a baby (2 Kings 4:17). The woman was rich, but she had no son. She gave birth to a baby boy as Elisha had promised.

22. c. setting up a room for him to stay in when he visited (2 Kings 4:10).

23. True (2 Kings 4:18–37).

24. a. brought the boy back from the dead (2 Kings 4:18–37).

26. This miracle might make you think of Jesus feeding five thousand men, plus untold women and children, with the contents of a small boy's lunch. Read about it in Matthew 14:13–21, Mark 6:30–44, Luke 9:10–17, and John 6:1–14.

27. True (2 Kings 4:38–41). There had been a famine, so food was scarce. The cook used poisonous gourds by mistake. Elisha made the stew pure so they could eat it.

28. False (2 Kings 5:1). Naaman was a respected Syrian commander.

29. a. leprosy (2 Kings 5:1).

30. A servant girl suggested that Elisha could cure Naaman (2 Kings 5:2–3).

32. c. *I do not have the power of God! The Syrian king wants to quarrel with me* (2 Kings 5:7).

33. True (2 Kings 5:8).

34. a. wash seven times in the Jordan River (2 Kings 5:10).

35. b. was angry (2 Kings 5:11). He did not understand why he could not wash himself in a river in Damascus and become cured there.

36. False. Naaman was cured as soon as he rose from bathing in the Jordan River the seventh time (2 Kings 5:14).

37. Naaman vowed to worship Elisha's God (2 Kings 5:18).

39. d. two mule loads (2 Kings 5:17).

41. True (2 Kings 5:22).

42. Yes. Naaman gave Gehazi six thousand pieces of silver rather than the three thousand he asked for, plus the two changes of clothes that Gehazi requested (2 Kings 5:23).

43. False (2 Kings 5:26). Elisha rebuked him for his greed.

44. d. said that Gehazi and his family would always be plagued with leprosy (2 Kings 5:27). Elisha probably reacted this way because the servant's greed had left a bad mark on Elisha's prophetic ministry.

    The fact that Naaman was happy to pay handsomely to be rid of his leprosy shows how great a punishment Gehazi and his family would suffer.

A Visit From the Queen

1. The story of the queen's visit can be found in the Old Testament.

2. d. Sheba (1 Kings 10:1 and 2 Chronicles 9:1).

3. a. she had heard of his fame (1 Kings 10:1 and 2 Chronicles 9:1).

6. True (1 Kings 10:1 and 2 Chronicles 9:1).

7. d. unknown. Her questions are not recorded in the Bible. Some scholars believe they may have been puzzling riddles designed to stump Solomon.

8. a. wisdom and sacrifices to God (1 Kings 10:4–5 and 2 Chronicles 9:3–4).

9. c. riches, palace, food, and servants (1 Kings 10:4–5 and 2 Chronicles 9:3–4).

10. False. The queen told Solomon she was amazed that he possessed twice as much wisdom as she had been told (1 Kings 10:7 and 2 Chronicles 9:6).

11. True (1 Kings 10:9 and 2 Chronicles 9:8).

12. Because she was from a foreign land, it is assumed the Queen of Sheba worshipped pagan gods rather than the God of Israel. When she saw Solomon's riches and heard his wisdom, she considered him blessed by God, causing her to praise Him. Christians today are witnesses for Jesus Christ. However, Jesus asks us to live a life of love and forgiveness under His grace rather than displaying vast wealth.

14. The total is 49,950 pounds. This is about the same weight as twelve Mercury Villager minivans.

NEHEMIAH BUILDS A WALL

1. The book of Nehemiah is found in the Old Testament.

2. As the title suggests, the book was written by Nehemiah.

4. c. suffering (Nehemiah 1:3).

5. False. The walls had been destroyed, which is why Nehemiah was called upon to undertake building the wall.

6. True (Nehemiah 1:11).

7. a. wept and prayed to God (Nehemiah 1:4–11).

8. b. cup bearer (Nehemiah 2:2). This was an important position that put Nehemiah in the king's presence every day.

9. b. looked sad (Nehemiah 2:3). Nehemiah had never before looked sad, so the king asked him if he was sick. Nehemiah told the king his people were unhappy.

10. c. go back and rebuild the city of Jerusalem (Nehemiah 2:5).

11. Yes, the king granted Nehemiah's request (Nehemiah 2:7).

12. True (Nehemiah 2:3).

14. b. his donkey (Nehemiah 2:12).

15. True (Nehemiah 2:19).

16. Nehemiah counted on God (Nehemiah 2:20).

18. d. the sheep gate (Nehemiah 3:1 and 3:32).

19. False. In fact, people tried to stop the work many times. Enemies made fun of the wall builders (Nehemiah 2:19 and 4:1–3); they threatened an attack (Nehemiah 4:7–23); enemies tried to distract Nehemiah from the project (Nehemiah 6:1–4); people tried to ruin Nehemiah's reputation (Nehemiah 6:5–9 and 10–14); finally, letters were sent to Nehemiah to scare him into stopping the project (Nehemiah 6:17–19).

20. False. He prayed to God, and the enemies' plans to sabotage the project were halted (Nehemiah 4:14–15).

22. a. they were too poor to feed their families (Nehemiah 5:2).

23. c. the rich Jews were taking advantage of their poor relatives (Nehemiah 5:7). They were forcing them to pay high taxes. They also loaned them money to be paid back with interest, a practice that was against the Jewish religion. Some people were so poor that they had to sell themselves into slavery (Nehemiah 5:4–6).

24. True (Nehemiah 5:12).

26. b. shook his sash (Nehemiah 5:13).

27. Yes (Nehemiah 5:13).

28. False: Nehemiah did not tax his people or buy property for himself (Nehemiah 5:15–16).

29. Nehemiah knew that the people already had enough burdens without him claiming a large amount of money and land for himself (Nehemiah 5:18). This is in contrast to the way the rich Jews were treating their relatives in Jerusalem.

30. The wall took fifty-two days to complete (Nehemiah 6:15).

LAMENTATIONS

1. The book of Lamentations is found in the Old Testament after the book of Jeremiah.

2. a. being sorry about something.

4. d. the destruction of Jerusalem in 586 BC.

6. True (Lamentations 1).

7. b. anger (Lamentations 2).

8. True (Lamentations 3:57–58).

9. True (Lamentations 5).

2. The name of Hosea's wife was Gomer (Hosea 1:3).

3. Jezreel (Hosea 1:4), Jezreel (Hosea 1:5).

5. house of Israel (Hosea 1:6).

6. True (Hosea 1:9).

7. No. There would come a time when Israel would be loved again by God (Hosea 1:10–11).

8. False. She was unfaithful to Hosea, just as Israel was unfaithful to God (Hosea 2:2–13).

9. c. win Gomer back (Hosea 2:14–17).

10. Gomer's unfaithfulness to Hosea is like Israel's unfaithfulness to God because, just as a husband wants his wife to love him, God wanted Israel to love Him.

11. God says He will become close to Israel and will show Israel great love. In return, Israel will love Him (Hosea 2:19–23).

12. False. He said they did not remember Him or accept His teachings (Hosea 4:6).

13. b. worshipping other gods (Hosea 4:10–13).

14. God was angry at Judah (Hosea 5:10).

15. a. invading and oppressing Israel (Hosea 5:10).

16. True (Hosea 5:15).

17. God says He wants love from His people (Hosea 6:5).

18. d. half-baked loaf of bread (Hosea 7:8). This means they rely too much on foreigners (verse 9) instead of God.

19. God says the nation of Israel is like a silly dove (Hosea 7:11).

20. d. flitting from place to place (Hosea 7:12). This means that the Israelites cannot decide what to do. They go from one country to another, seeking help.

22. True (Hosea 8:1–14).

23. Returning to Egypt meant returning to a life of slavery. The story about how God released the Israelites from slavery in Egypt can be found in Exodus 1–14.

24. b. calves (Hosea 13:2).

25. True (Hosea 14:1).

26. d. forgive their sins (Hosea 14:2).

28. They promise not to worship other gods (Hosea 14:3).

29. a. a new life (Hosea 14:4–8).

30. John 3:16 says: "For God so loved the world, that he gave his only begotten Son, that whosoever believeth in him should not perish, but have everlasting life" (King James Version).

JOEL

2. Joel wrote the book of Joel.

3. a. the Old Testament, after Hosea.

4. b. prophet.

5. True.

6. b. locusts (Joel 1:4).

7. True (Joel 1:4). A plague of locusts had invaded the land.

8. b. repent of their sins (Joel 2:12).

9. True (Joel 2:18–19).

10. True (Joel 2:21–23).

11. The people should be glad because of what God had done for them. They will have plenty to eat and will never be hated again (Joel 2:25–27).

12. False. God will judge the nations in the Valley of Jehoshaphat (Joel 3:2).

14. d. Judah (Joel 3:19).

15. **The Lord will live on Mount Zion (Joel 3:21).**

2. As its name suggests, Micah wrote the book of Micah.

3. a. Old Testament, after the book of Jonah.

4. True.

5. b. idolatry (Micah 1:5).

6. Micah said Samaria would lie in ruins (Micah 1:6).

7. d. walking naked and howling (Micah 1:8).

8. False (Micah 1:9).

9. The people did not like Micah's prophecy because they did not want to hear about being punished. They wanted to hear that they were good and they could do anything they wanted (Micah 2:6–11).

10. a. lie (Micah 2:11).

11. False. He said the rulers were evil (Micah 3:1).

13. True.

15. a. they thought the Lord was with them (Micah 3:11).

16. True (Micah 4:5).

17. This ruler is Jesus (Micah 5:2).

18. False: Bethlehem was a small town, yet it is the birthplace of Jesus.

20. a. Assyria (Micah 5:6).

21. False. God wants us to have a relationship with Him (Micah 6:8).

22. False. Evil people will get no joy from their earthly treasures. The Lord hates for people to get things by being dishonest (6:9–16).

1. The Bible has four Gospels: Matthew, Mark, Luke, and John.

2. a. first part of the New Testament.

3. A concordance is a list of words you can find in certain Bible verses. For instance, if you want to find out where the Bible talks about love, you can look up the word "love" in a concordance. The concordance should have a list of verses with the word "love" in them. Look in the back of your Bible. Does it have a concordance? You can use it the next time you want to find a verse. The concordance in the back of your Bible will not be complete because a complete concordance would make your Bible too big to carry to church. A big book called an exhaustive concordance will list every verse and word, and might be a good study tool to help you learn even more about your Bible.

4. c. Matthew, Mark, Luke, and John.

5. a. the life and ministry of Jesus.

6. The red letters mean that those words were spoken by Jesus Himself. Many King James Version Bibles print Jesus' words in red. Some new versions do not.

7. b. the Acts of the Apostles and Revelation (Acts 1:4–5, 8–9, 9:4–6, 10–12, 15–16; 11:16; 18:9–10; 20:35; 22:7–8, 10, 18, 21; 23:11; 26:14–18, and Revelation 1:8, 11; 1:17–3:22; 22:7, 12–13, 16, 20).

8. False. Although Jesus is quoted in all four Gospels, He did not actually write any part of them.

10. b. collected taxes for Rome.

11. Matthew traced Jesus' lineage back to King David because he wanted to show us that Jesus is King. Jesus is worthy of our worship.

13. True.

14. Although it is not the longest Gospel, the book of Matthew is the Gospel with the greatest number of chapters.

THE BIRTH OF JESUS

1. True. The story of Jesus' birth is also found in Luke.

3. b. Joseph (Matthew 1:18).

5. An angel of the Lord first told Mary she would have a baby (Luke 1:28–33).

6. True (Luke 1:39–40).

7. True (Matthew 1:20).

9. Jesus was born in Bethlehem (Luke 2:5–7).

10. b. a census was being taken (Luke 2:1–3). A census is a count of how many people are living in a place at a certain time in history. The United States government takes a census of everyone in the country every ten years. Looking at old census records is one way to find out about your own ancestors.

11. False. King Herod was jealous of the new baby because Jesus was called King of the Jews (Matthew 2:1–3).

13. a. gold, frankincense, and myrrh
(Matthew 2:11).

14. False. There was no room for them in the
inn (Luke 2:7).

15. c. angels (Luke 2:8–14).

17. False. God warned them in a dream not
to go back to King Herod. They returned
to their country by another road
(Matthew 2:12).

18. False. She had been told what to name
Jesus (Luke 2:21).

19. a. Egypt (Matthew 2:13).

20. d. died (Matthew 2:14–15).

22. Nazarene (Matthew 2:23). This is in keeping with the word of the prophets about
the Messiah.

24. c. it was required by Mosaic Law (Luke
2:24). The freedom we enjoy as Christians
did not come about until after Jesus' ministry and resurrection.

25. Simeon (Luke 2:25). Upon seeing the baby, Simeon told Mary and Joseph that Jesus was the Messiah.

26. b. Jerusalem (Luke 2:22).

27. True. He was proclaimed the Messiah by Simeon, and also Anna the prophetess (Luke 2:22–38).

2. True.

3. d. Nazareth (Luke 2:39).

4. c. Passover (Luke 2:45).

5. It took Mary and Joseph three days to find Jesus (Luke 2:45).

6. a. in the Temple, amazing the teachers with His wisdom (Luke 2:46).

7. True (Luke 2:49). He answered them, "How is it that you sought me? Wist ye not that I must be about my Father's business?" (King James Version). This means, "Why did you look for me? Didn't you know I was doing my Father's work?"

8. a. John the Baptist. Before John the Baptist was born, he jumped for joy upon hearing of Jesus' impending birth (Luke 1:41). He baptized Jesus (Matthew 3:13–17; Mark 1:9–11; Luke 3:21–22; John 1:31–34). Jesus spoke about John the Baptist after John's death (Matthew 11:12–19; Luke 7:19–35).

10. d. locusts and wild honey (Mark 1:6).

11. True (Matthew 3:11–12).

12. True (Mark 1:8).

13. c. was evil (Luke 3:19).

14. He was put into prison (Luke 3:20).

15. John the Baptist (Matthew 3:13–17; Mark 1:9–11; Luke 3:21–22; John 1:31–34).

16. d. a dove (Luke 3:21–22).

17. False. Instead, Jesus told Satan that people need more than bread. They also need God's word (Matthew 4:4).

18. c. Jesus was very hungry and wanted to eat because He had not eaten for forty days (Matthew 4:1–3). Satan thought Jesus' hunger would cause Him to give in to this temptation. Satan was mistaken.

20. If you think that Satan challenged Jesus in these ways to see whether Jesus was prideful, you are probably right. Pride is responsible for many sins. Satan often uses human pride in his tests. By telling

Jesus He could prove He was God's Son by performing miracles, Satan hoped Jesus' pride would cause Him to fail the tests. By resisting Satan, Jesus showed us that God is more important than our own pride.

21. True (Matthew 4:5–7).

22. a. all the world's kingdoms (Matthew 4:9).

23. Angels helped Jesus after He was tempted by Satan.

25. Jesus began His ministry in Galilee (Luke 4:14).

JESUS HEALS THE SICK

1. a. the Gospels.

3. False. He told the man not to tell anyone, but to go directly to the priest and offer the sacrifice required under Moses' law (Matthew 8:1–4).

4. d. giving an order for him to be healed (Matthew 8:5–13 and Luke 7:1–10). Jesus healed the officer's servant merely by ordering him to get well. This was unusual because Jesus did not even enter the officer's house to see or touch the servant.

6. Jesus healed Peter's mother-in-law (Matthew 8:14–15). Peter is called Simon in Mark 1:30–31 and Luke 4:38–39, which also give account of this particular healing.

7. b. touching her hand (Matthew 8:14–15, Mark 1:30–31, Luke 4:38–39).

9. True (Luke 4:41).

10. False. Jesus gave the demons an order not to speak, because He did not want them to tell who He was (Luke 4:41).

11. a. herd of pigs (Matthew 8:28–34, Mark 5:1–20, Luke 8:26–39).

12. b. were afraid (Mark 5:15, Luke 8:35).

13. True (Matthew 8:34, Mark 5:17, Luke 8:37).

14. After the man was healed, he wanted to go with Jesus (Mark 5:18, Luke 8:38).

15. True (Mark 5:19, Luke 8:39).

16. Yes (Mark 5:20).

17. a. cloak (Matthew 9:20, Mark 5:28, Luke 8:44).

18. d. faith (Matthew 9:22, Mark 5:34, Luke 8:48).

20. True (Matthew 9:23). In fact, preparations were already being made for her funeral.

21. sleeping (Matthew 9:24, Mark 5:39, Luke 8:52).

22. b. two blind men (Matthew 9:27–29).

23. Jesus told them not to tell anyone (Matthew 9:30).

24. No. Word of the healing spread everywhere (Matthew 9:31).

1. Luke's Gospel is the third book in the New Testament.

3. The Acts of the Apostles is the fifth book in the New Testament.

4. True.

5. The four Gospels are: Matthew, Mark, Luke, John.

6. True. You can read about them in the Gospels. Some of them are recorded in Luke 4:31–5:26 and 6:6–19.

7. a. tax collectors and outcasts (Luke 5:30). Some religious leaders in Jesus' day did not understand why the Messiah would spend time with tax collectors and outcasts. In Jesus' day, tax collectors often kept much of the tax money for themselves and were thought to be stealing from others.

8. True (Luke 6:1–5). Some Pharisees were upset with Jesus' disciples for picking wheat to eat on the Sabbath. Jesus told them King David had fed his hungry

troops rather than stick to a strict religious rule. It was hard for the Pharisees to argue with Jesus about this, since King David was a hero. Jesus' point was that people are more important than following rules.

9. c. a man with a paralyzed hand (Luke 6:6–10). Although Jesus knew He was being watched by enemies who were hoping He would break the Jewish law about the Sabbath, Jesus healed the man anyway. Jesus said it was lawful to do good on the Sabbath. Again, this showed how Jesus valued people more than rules.

10. False (Luke 6:11). Jesus' enemies were angry that He had broken the Jewish law.

11. a. follower.

12. Jesus' disciples are named in Luke 6:12–16. They are:
    Simon, whom He named Peter
    Andrew, Simon's brother
    James
    John
    Philip
    Bartholomew
    Matthew

Thomas
James, son of Alphaeus
Simon, who was called the Patriot
   (or the Zealot)
Judas, son of James
Judas Iscariot, who became the traitor.

13. Soon after he chose His disciples, Jesus
   preached the Sermon on the Mount, also
   known as the Beatitudes (Luke 6:20–26).

14. False. Jesus said we should love our enemies (Luke 6:27).

16. The Golden Rule says to do unto others
   as you would have them do unto you.
   This means you should treat everyone
   else the same way you would like them
   to treat you.

17. False (Luke 6:37–42). We should be care-
   ful about how we judge other people,
   because God will judge us by the same
   standards we use for others.

18. a. washed His feet with her tears (Luke
   7:36–37).

19. d. said that Jesus shouldn't let a sinful
   woman touch Him (Luke 7:39).

20. True (Luke 7:47).

21. Jesus said, "Thy sins are forgiven," and "Thy faith hath saved thee; go in peace" (Luke 7:48).

22. False. Luke names several women who followed Jesus, including Mary Magdalene, Joanna, Susanna, and other unnamed women (Luke 8:1–3).

Luke Tells Us What Jesus Said

1. A parable is a lesson told in story form.

2. d. His disciples could understand them,
    but not everyone else (Luke 8:10). Jesus
    did not want to share His knowledge
    with everyone, only those who truly
    wanted to follow Him.

3. False. Jesus said that His family are those
    who hear and obey God (Luke 8:21).
    This does not mean we are not to love
    and honor our families, but that we are
    to be close to people who love the Lord,
    whether or not they are family members.

4. a. John the Baptist (Luke 9:7–9, 18, 20).
    John the Baptist was a cousin of Jesus
    whose ministry was legendary. Some
    people also thought that Jesus was
    Elijah or another prophet come back to
    life.

5. *Resurrected* means "brought back to life
    from the dead."

6. True (Luke 9:21–22).

9. d. Moses and Elijah (Luke 9:31). This was amazing because both Moses and Elijah had long been dead.

10. Jesus' visitors talked to Him about how He would soon fulfill God's plan for Him (Luke 9:31).

12. b. were afraid and told no one (Luke 9:36).

13. True (Luke 9:46).

14. Jesus said that the person who is the least important on earth is the most important person in heaven. This is an important teaching of Jesus because it is the opposite of what the world teaches and it even goes against our own human nature. Rather than looking to be the most important person in the world, it is better for us to put Jesus first.

15. a. told him to stop (Luke 9:49). They were upset because he was not part of their group.

16. Jesus said, "Forbid him not; for he that is not against us is for us" (Luke 9:50). This means Jesus welcomes all who love Him, not just people who belong to a certain group.

18. False. The Samaritan village did not want Jesus to come through there because He was on His way to Jerusalem. James and John asked Jesus if He wanted them to command fire to come from heaven to destroy the village (Luke 9:54).

19. c. not to be unforgiving toward the citizens of the town. He said, "Ye know not what manner of spirit ye are of; For the Son of man is not come to destroy men's lives, but to save them" (Luke 9:55–56). This means He told the disciples not to be so mean-spirited. Jesus wants to save us.

20. False. Jesus and the disciples went another way (Luke 9:56).

22. d. nothing (Luke 10:4).

23. The workers would be taken care of by the people in each town. They were told to go to a house and greet the people living there with peace. Those people were to give them food and shelter during their stay in the town.

24. a. lambs among wolves (Luke 10:3).

25. True (Luke 10:17).

THE PRODIGAL SON

1. Jesus told the story of the prodigal son.

2. You can find the story of the prodigal son in Luke 15:11–32.

3. False.

4. The word *prodigal* means "recklessly extravagant; lavish."

5. The wealthy man had two sons (Luke 15:11).

6. a. give him his share of his inheritance (Luke 15:12).

7. b. property that is passed on when someone dies.

8. True (Luke 15:11–13).

9. c. wasted his money (Luke 15:13).

10. d. tending pigs (Luke 15:15).

12. False. The father ran to the son, hugged him, and kissed him (Luke 15:20).

13. d. a ring, a robe, and shoes (Luke 15:22).

14. True (Luke 15:23–24).

15. False. He begged the older brother to join the party (Luke 15:28).

16. d. was angry (Luke 15:28).

17. He was upset because he had not been rewarded with a party, even though he had been faithful and had never strayed from the father (Luke 29–30).

18. c. "Everything I have is yours and we are close" (Luke 15: 31).

19. True (Luke 15:32). The younger brother had been lost, but was found. He had been dead, but was alive.

THE GOOD SAMARITAN

1. You can find the story of the Good Samaritan in Luke 10:25–37.

2. False: The parable of the Good Samaritan can be found only in Luke.

4. c. a story that teaches a lesson.

5. d. "Who is my neighbor?" (Luke 10:29).

6. a. a lawyer (Luke 10:25).

7. c. had been beaten and robbed (Luke 10:30).

8. False (Luke 10:31–32).

9. The man was on his way from Jerusalem to Jericho (Luke 10:30).

10. The Samaritan stopped to help the injured man (Luke 10:33).

13. c. oil and wine (Luke 10:34).

14. True (Luke 10:35).

15. c. an inn (Luke 10:34).

16. The Samaritan give the innkeeper two denarii (Luke 10:35).

18. True. The lawyer said the neighbor was the person who showed mercy (Luke 10:36).

19. The Samaritan acted as a neighbor.

20. d. "Go and do likewise" (Luke 10:37). This means we should be kind to people in need whether or not they belong to our group.

JESUS' RESURRECTION

1. True. Although all four Gospels don't talk about everything that happened to Jesus, all do record His resurrection (Matthew 28:1–15; Mark 16:1–11; Luke 24: 1–12; John 20:1–18).

2. Matthew 28:1 names Mary Magdalene, Mary the mother of James, and Salome. There were other unnamed women. Luke 24:10 names Joanna.

3. a. an angel of the Lord (Matthew 28:2).

4. c. "Fear not, for Jesus has risen" (Matthew 28:5–6). Note: An earthquake had already happened when the angel rolled away the stone (Matthew 28:2).

5. False (Luke 24:11). They thought the women were telling idle tales.

6. Jesus' disciples Peter and John went to the grave. The King James Version refers to John as "the other disciple whom Jesus loved" (John 20:2–4).

7. True (John 20:11–18).

8. c. "Peace be unto you" (John 20:19).

9. c. wanted to reassure them (John 20:19).
   They were hiding because they feared
   they would be killed for following Jesus.

2. The Lord's Prayer appears in both Luke and Matthew. The version from Matthew 6:9–13 is quoted here from the King James Version because it is the more complete of the two:

> Our Father, who art in heaven, Hallowed by thy name. Thy Kingdom come. Thy will be done in earth, as it is in heaven. Give us this day our daily bread. And forgive us our debts as we forgive our debtors. And lead us not into temptation, but deliver us from evil. For thine is the kingdom, and the power, and the glory, forever and ever. Amen.

3. a. one of them had asked Him to teach them how to pray (Luke 11:1).

4. God is in heaven.

5. He means that we should respect, honor, and revere God's holy name.

7. True.

8. True (Matthew 6:5).

9. A hypocrite is a person who acts like someone good in public but does evil things when no one else is watching.

11. False. The Lord's Prayer is a model for us to go by. However, sharing our own concerns with God helps us to become closer to Him. God loves you and He wants to hear about your cares. He also likes for you to thank Him for His goodness.

13. This prayer is named the Lord's Prayer because Jesus taught it to us.

14. d. God will forgive us when we forgive others (Matthew 6:14–15).

15. False. Those who pray in the open to get praise already have their reward (Matthew 6:16).

PAUL SPEAKS ABOUT LOVE

1. The Apostle Paul wrote 1 Corinthians.

2. b. members of the church at Corinth. Paul's letters to them gave advice on how they should live as Christians.

4. False. Without love, any speech is just a lot of noise (1 Corinthians 13:1).

5. d. none of the above. You must have love (1 Corinthians 13:2–3).

6. d. proud (1 Corinthians 13:4). This means you will let the person you love be first, or the most important.

7. This means if you love someone, it will take a lot to make you mad at that person.

8. False (1 Corinthians 13:8–9).

9. Love is the greatest (1 Corinthians 13:13).

1. c. a set of attitudes you'll have if you love God.

2. We can learn about the fruit of the Spirit in Galatians 5:22–26.

3. The apostle Paul told us about the fruit of the Spirit.

4. a. members of a group of churches in Galatia.

6. Paul speaks of love in 1 Corinthians 13.

7. b. happiness in the Lord.

9. c. you can forgive other people when they sin against you.

11. True (Galatians 5:22).

12. False. No matter what, a person of faith always believes in God (Hebrews 11:1).

13. c. strong, but kind to others.

14. d. controlling yourself and not going to the extreme.

15. False. He wanted to show that Christian conduct is more important than following the law (Galatians 5:18).

16. d. don't think about their bodies as much as they think about living for Christ (Galatians 5:25).

17. a. we obey Christ (Galatians 5:25).

18. False. Christians should not seek others' possessions (Galatians 5:26).

19. There are many good reasons to obey Christ. In this passage, Paul is showing us how we will act if we are obedient. Loving others is a good way to be an ambassador for Christ.

20. The nine elements of the fruit of the Spirit are love, joy, peace, long-suffering, gentleness, goodness, faith, meekness, and temperance.

1. a. Peter.

2. True.

3. b. is named first in every list of the apostles in the Bible. These lists are found in Matthew 10:2–4, Mark 3:13–19, Luke 6:12–16 and Acts 1:13–14.

4. b. persecuted Christians (1 Peter 1:1).

5. d. eternal life. The Christian looks forward to living with God in heaven rather than having lots of things here.

6. True (1 Peter 1:14). Jesus' teachings go against the world's system of greed and materialism. Instead of encouraging us to get more stuff, He tells us God will provide our needs. When we trust God, there is no need to be greedy or to wish we had more than someone else.

7. *Redeemed* means "saved." Those who accept Jesus' gift of salvation are saved and forgiven for their sins.

8. a. Jesus (1 Peter 1:7). Jesus redeemed us when He was crucified on the cross.

9. Thou shalt not covet (Exodus 20:17). We should not be jealous of other people's things or accomplishments, but be happy for them in their success. When you are jealous of someone, think about everything God has done for you.

10. The warning to put aside evil speaking might remind us of the commandment not to bear false witness against our neighbor, or not to tell lies (Exodus 20:16).

11. a. newborn babes (1 Peter 2:2). This means we should desire the pure milk of the Word, which is the Word of God.

12. d. make Christians grow (1 Peter 2:2). The more we read the Bible, the more we learn about Jesus and the Christian faith.

13. c. living stones (1 Peter 2:5).

14. True (1 Peter 2:5).

16. True (1 Peter 2:7). This means Jesus is the foundation of our faith.

17. This means people who don't want to obey Jesus will trip over His Word and find it insulting and offensive.

18. True (1 Peter 2:11–12). We are ambassa-
dors for Christ. Our conduct should cause
unbelievers to praise the Lord.

19. A sojourner is a guest. We are guests in
this world, because our true home is in
heaven with the Lord. We can enjoy
God's awesome creation while we live
here.

20. False (1 Peter 2:11). He means Christians
are not at home in this world.

21. b. obey the laws of their nations (1 Peter
2:13). If we obey the law, no one can say
we think we are above the law. Christians
are obligated to be good citizens.

22. False (1 Peter 2:18). We are to forgive
others.

23. a. remember how Jesus trusted God
(1 Peter 2:23–24). Jesus did not insult
people who insulted him. He trusted God.

24. c. lost sheep (1 Peter 2:25). This means
they were sinners who had gotten away
from God.

25. The three parables are about the lost sheep (Matthew 18:12–14 and Luke 15:3–7); the lost son (Luke 15:11–32); and the lost coin (Luke 15:8–10).

26. Psalm 23 refers to Jesus as a shepherd.

27. *Submit* means to comply, to obey, or to go along with someone.

28. False (1 Peter 3:1). The wife should submit to her husband, even if he does not obey Christ. This does not mean the wife is a slave to the husband or that she should be mistreated, but that she should honor her marriage vows. Because the Christian church was just beginning to take hold in the world at the time Peter wrote this letter, some women who proclaimed Christ were already married to men who practiced pagan religions. By giving this instruction, Peter was discouraging these women from divorce.

30. False (1 Peter 3:3–4). Beauty from within is precious to God.

31. d. honor their wives (1 Peter 3:7).

32. a. not as strong physically as her husband (1 Peter 3:7). This does not mean the woman is not as good as the man or inferior to him; it just means that she is not as muscular or as strong in the body. He was encouraging husbands to look out for their wives' best interests and to protect them.

33. True (1 Peter 3:7).

34. True (1 Peter 3:14). Peter wrote this to encourage Christians who were suffering just for being Christians. Some important people in the government did not like Christians, and they tried to make their lives difficult. Sometimes people were even killed for being Christians.

35. b. meekness (1 Peter 3:15–16).

36. The Sermon on the Mount, where He preached the Beatitudes (Matthew 5:1–12 and Luke 6:20–26).

38. d. when you love people, you can forget about their sins (1 Peter 4:8). It is easier to forgive someone you love than someone you hate.

39. True (1 Peter 4:15).

40. a. be busybodies.

41. Our earthly shepherds in the church today are elders of the church, or pastors (1 Peter 5:1).

42. b. elders (1 Peter 5:5).

43. God wants us to respect our parents. They can teach us a lot about life and how to be Christians.

44. The devil is the enemy of Christians (1 Peter 5:8).

45. "Amen" is the last word in 1 Peter (1 Peter 5:14).

1. We know that Peter is the author because he tells us in 2 Peter 1:1.

3. a. Christians in Asia Minor (2 Peter 1:1).

4. It is important to study all sixty-six books of the Bible. Peter's letters are important because they give us instructions on how to live as Christians.

5. True (2 Peter 1:3–4).

6. The traits a Christian should have are: faith, virtue, knowledge, self-control, perseverance, godliness, brotherly kindness, and love (2 Peter 1:5–7). Can you think of someone who is like this? Think about how Christians can display these characteristics in real life.

8. c. die (2 Peter 1:14). The New King James Version calls the tabernacle a tent. This is symbolic of how short life on earth is in comparison to eternal life with God. Few people live in a tent all their lives on earth. Likewise, we live in our bodies for a time until we go and live with God in heaven.

9. True (2 Peter 1:16–18).

10. False. False prophets will be punished (2 Peter 2:12–13).

11. d. all of the above (2 Peter 2:1–3).

12. a. a talking donkey (2 Peter 2:15).

13. Peter means that people who are not truly devoted to the Lord may seem to be faithful for a while but will sooner or later return to their wicked ways.

14. b. as a thief in the night (2 Peter 3:10). This means it will be unexpected. Do not listen to anyone who claims to know the exact day the Lord will return. Not even Jesus knows this day (Matthew 24:36).

15. True. We must stay faithful to God's Word (2 Peter 3:17).